PREKINDERGARTEN– GRADE 2

Mathematics Assessment Sampler

Mathematics Assessment Samplers

A series edited by Anne M. Collins

PREKINDERGARTEN— GRADE 2

Mathematics Assessment Sampler

Items Aligned with NCTM's
Principles and Standards for School Mathematics

DeAnn Huinker, *Editor*
University of Wisconsin, Madison, Wisconsin

Anne M. Collins, *Series Editor*
Lesley University, Cambridge, Massachusetts

WRITING TEAM
Lynn M. McGarvey
Gladis Kersaint
Linda Landin
Rebeka Salemi

NCTM

NATIONAL COUNCIL OF
TEACHERS OF MATHEMATICS

Copyright © 2006 by
THE NATIONAL COUNCIL OF TEACHERS OF MATHEMATICS, INC.
1906 Association Drive, Reston, VA 20191-1502
(703) 620-9840; (800) 235-7566; www.nctm.org

Library of Congress Cataloging-in-Publication Data

Huinker, DeAnn.
  Mathematics assessment sampler, prekindergarten–grade 2 : items aligned with nctm's principles and standards for school mathematics / DeAnn Huinker, Anne M. Collins, Lynn M. McGarvey.
      p. cm. — (Mathematics assessment samplers)
  Includes bibliographical references.
  ISBN 0-87353-591-X
  1. Mathematics—Study and teaching (Preschool) 2. Mathematics—Study and teaching (Primary) 3. Mathematical ability—Testing. I. Collins, Anne M., 1944– II. McGarvey, Lynn M. III. Title. IV. Series.
  QA11.2.H85 2006
  372.7'044—dc22
                                    2006010750

The National Council of Teachers of Mathematics is a public voice of mathematics education, providing vision, leadership, and professional development to support teachers in ensuring mathematics learning of the highest quality for all students.

PRINTED IN THE UNITED STATES OF AMERICA

Contents

On the Cover vi

Preface vii

Acknowledgments ix

About This Series xi

Introduction: About This Book 1

Chapter 1: Number and Operations 5

Chapter 2: Algebra 51

Chapter 3: Geometry 85

Chapter 4: Measurement 117

Chapter 5: Data Analysis and Probability 153

Blackline Masters 199

Appendix: Items Matrices 231

Bibliography 237

Sources for Assessment Items 239

On the Cover

The term *sampler* comes from the Latin *exemplum*, meaning "an example to be followed, a pattern, a model or example." The earliest known samplers date to the sixteenth century, although samplers were probably stitched long before that time. Beginning in the mid–eighteenth century, young girls commonly worked samplers as part of their education. During Victorian times, samplers metamorphosed into decorative articles hung by proud parents on parlor walls. As designs became more elaborate, generally only one stitch remained in use, leading to the well–known cross–stitch samplers of today.

The electronically "stitched" sampler on the cover highlights the relationships among knowledge (owl), learning (school), and the NCTM Standards (logo). The number patterns embedded in the border design (the counting sequence across the top; the Fibonacci sequence, 1, 1, 2, 3, 5, 8, ..., around the left, bottom, and right borders) echo pattern motifs seen in samplers in earlier times.

The Mathematics Assessment Samplers are intended to give teachers examples—not exhaustive listings—of assessment items that reveal what students know and can do in mathematics, that pinpoint areas of strengths and weakness in students' mathematical knowledge, and that shape teachers' curricular and instructional decisions toward the goal of maximizing all students' understanding of mathematics.

Preface

The National Council of Teachers of Mathematics asked our task force to compile a collection of assessment items that support *Principles and Standards for School Mathematics* (NCTM 2000). This book, one of four in the series, focuses on classroom assessment in prekindergarten–grade 2. The other three books, for teachers in grades 3–5, grades 6–8, and grades 9–12, also contain practical examples and samples of student work aligned with the NCTM Standards. Each of those books contains multiple-choice, short-response, and extended-response questions designed to help classroom teachers identify problems specifically related to NCTM Standards and Expectations. A helpful matrix that summarizes this information is contained in the appendix of each volume. Because many young children are in the prereading and prewriting stages of development, this Assessment Sampler for prekindergarten through grade 2 does not rely on written student responses. Rather, it emphasizes the need for observations, interviews, and performance assessments as means for teachers to assess their students in the early grades.

The NCTM *Assessment Standards for School Mathematics* (1995) document identifies the role of classroom assessment as one that should—

- provide a rich variety of mathematical topics and problem situations,
- give students opportunities to investigate problems in many ways,
- question and listen to students,
- look for evidence of learning from many sources, and
- expect students to use concepts and procedures effectively in solving problems.

Our task force faced a special challenge. Because not many resources are available for assessing very young children, members of the task force wrote and pilot-tested a variety of assessments. We depended on interviews, observations, and performance assessments as our primary criteria for determining what the young children in the pilot tests knew and were able to do. One advantage to using observations, interviews, and performance assessments is being able to listen to children as they verbalize their thinking. Student reasoning fosters invaluable insights into what students understand and in which areas of mathematics they need more experience. Listening to and observing students working through mathematical tasks give teachers ongoing opportunities to make instructional decisions and refine the structure of their lessons accordingly.

We encourage you to use the items contained in this Assessment Sampler with your own students. As you work toward extending your own classroom repertoire of assessment items, we hope you find the bibliography and resources sections helpful in your pursuit.

Acknowledgments

The editors and writing team wish to thank the educators listed below for their suggestions, contributions of student work, reviews, and general assistance.

Johanna Barron
Chris Brown
Davida Burks
Debbie Carpenito
Barbara Charles
Linda Dacey
Challa Goedeke
Carole Greenes
Melissa Hedges
Jane Jackson
Mary Keane
SueAnn Kearns
Grazyna Klimek
Karen LaRone
Sarah Marcus

Erin Martin
Jennifer Mastrullo
Vicki Milstein
Angela Murphy
Lee Ann Pruske
Jacqueline Pocklington
Nancy Sanchez
Rachel Scheff
Amy Shields
Meghan Steinmeyer
Glen Teal
Siobhan Theriault
Peggy Winchester
Cheri Wing-Jones

About This Series

An emphasis on assessment, testing, and gathering evidence of student achievement has become an educational phenomenon in recent years. In fact, we can fairly say that assessment is driving many educational decisions, including grade placement, graduation, and teacher evaluation. With that influence in mind, educators need to use good assessment material as an essential tool in the teaching and learning processes. Good problems are those that are mathematically rich, can be solved in multiple ways, promote critical thinking, and can be evaluated in a consistent manner—that is, teacher X and teacher Y would be likely to evaluate a problem in the same manner with the appropriate rubric.

Assessment is actually only one of three major considerations in the processes of teaching and learning. As such, assessment must be viewed in conjunction with curriculum and instruction. Just as a curriculum aligned with standards can guide instructional decisions, so too can assessment guide both instructional and curricular decisions. Therefore, items designed to assess specific standards and expectations should be incorporated into the classroom repertoire of assessment tasks.

In its *Assessment Standards for School Mathematics* (*Assessment Standards*), the National Council of Teachers of Mathematics (NCTM 1995) articulated four purposes for assessments and their results: (1) monitoring students' progress toward learning goals, (2) making instructional decisions, (3) evaluating students' achievement, and (4) evaluating programs. Further, the Assessment Principle in *Principles and Standards for School Mathematics* (*Principles and Standards*) states that "assessment should not merely be done *to* students; rather, it should be done *for* students" (NCTM 2000, p. 22). We have included a variety of rubrics in this series to assist the classroom teacher in providing feedback to students. Often, if students understand what is expected of them on individual extended-response problems, they tend to answer the questions more fully or provide greater detail than when they have no idea about the grading rubric being used.

This series was designed to present samples of student assessment items aligned with *Principles and Standards* (NCTM 2000). The items reflect the mathematics that all students should know and be able to do in grades prekindergarten–2, 3–5, 6–8, and 9–12. The items focus both on students' conceptual knowledge and on their procedural skills. The problems were designed as formative assessments, that is, assessments that help teachers learn how their students think about mathematical concepts, how students' understanding is communicated, and how such evidence can be used to guide instructional decisions.

The sample items contained in this publication are not a comprehensive set of examples but, rather, just a sampling. The problems are suitable for use as benchmark assessments or as evaluations of how well students have met particular NCTM Standards and

Expectations. Some student work is included with comments so that teachers can objectively examine a particular problem; study the way a student responded; and draw conclusions that, we hope, will translate into classroom practice.

NCTM's *Assessment Standards* (1995) indicates that (a) assessment should enhance mathematics learning, (b) assessment should promote equity, (c) assessment should be an open process, (d) assessment should promote valid inferences about mathematics learning, and (e) assessment should be a coherent process. This series presents problems and tasks that, when used as one component of the assessment process, help meet those Assessment Standards.

Introduction: About This Book

THIS SAMPLER provides assessment tasks that are appropriate for use with students from age 4 through age 8 (prekindergarten–grade 2). The intent of this book is to provide teachers of primary grades mathematics with samples of assessment tasks that reflect the various ways assessments can be used prior to, during, and following mathematics instruction. Although every classroom moment can be considered an assessment moment, teachers should at times deliberately plan and take opportunities to look more closely at the knowledge of individual students and to gain insights about the knowledge of the class as a whole. *Assessment Standards for School Mathematics* (NCTM 1995) identifies four purposes for assessment: (1) monitoring students' progress toward learning goals, (2) making instructional decisions, (3) evaluating students' achievement, and (4) evaluating programs. The expectation of this book is that teachers will consider the potential of these tasks to uncover the mathematical understandings of their students for the purpose of planning further instruction.

Gathering a collection of readily available assessment items at the prekindergarten–grade 2 level was not possible, particularly for some of the content strands. Therefore, the writing team created and adapted tasks, field-tested the tasks in classroom settings, and revised the tasks on the basis of the classroom experiences. Student work samples or anecdotal records from those experiences are included for each of the tasks. We encourage groups of teachers to work together to analyze and discuss students' work for the purpose of identifying instructional approaches to move both individual students and the entire class of students forward in, and increase the depth of, their understanding.

The writing team considered various issues and concerns in the development of each assessment task. Each assessment task was created to address some aspect of each of the NCTM Content Standards and to focus on particular Expectations. Each task assesses a varied range of Expectations within each of the Content Standards. More tasks are included for the Number and Operations and the Geometry strands than the other three strands because number and geometry comprise a major focus of mathematics at the prekindergarten–grade-2 level. An important consideration was to identify tasks that do not rely on a student's ability to read or write. Given the range of students' emerging reading and writing abilities, many of the tasks were created or adapted to permit the directions to be given orally and to allow for the use of concrete materials. During assessments, students may be involved in telling, recording, or showing, thereby requiring teachers to consider various methods for collecting information that captures evidence of students' understanding. That evidence allows teachers to measure and monitor the mathematical growth of individual students.

Student Action	Teacher Actions to Document Students' Understanding
Telling	Write notes, mark checklists, or make an audiotape or videotape of the student
Recording (e.g., writing, drawing, cutting, gluing, and using symbols)	Add written notes on students' written records to clarify what the student produced
Showing (e.g., producing results with concrete materials)	Take a picture of or sketch students' models

The difference between an assessment task and an instructional activity relates to the teacher's role in posing questions, listening to students' responses, and making judgments about students' understandings. The intent of the assessment tasks in this book is to focus on the task as a tool for gaining insights into students' mathematical knowledge. Each task has the potential for further development and could be used as a mathematics activity. The assessment tasks were designed as formative assessments, that is, to guide teachers in making informed instructional decisions. The tasks were designed to access a range of possible mathematical understandings. Each assessment task was developed not only to reveal what a student knows or does not yet know but also to gather information about how he or she knows that information.

This book contains five chapters. Each chapter focuses on a specific content strand: Number and Operations, Geometry, Measurement, Algebra, and Data Analysis and Probability. The authors list targeted Standards and Expectations for each task along with the intended grade range. In addition to the tasks and solutions, we include sections that—

- discuss the mathematics,
- suggest how teachers might use the tasks,
- identify the continuum of expected understanding,
- provide examples of student work, and
- suggest variations for adapting the task to a range of learners.

The "About the mathematics" sections describe the mathematical knowledge being assessed and what teachers might learn as a result of having students engage in the task. The "Using this assessment task" sections contain information on preparing for and using each task, for example, a list of the materials needed, a description of the delivery format, tips for implementation, and suggested additional prompts. Although we recommend a preferred format for delivery to allow the greatest access to students' understanding, teachers are the best judges of what format is most appropriate for their students. We use the wording "This task is designed to be used" to alert teachers that they may need to use alternative approaches if they decide to deliver tasks in alternative formats. The "Continuum of Understanding" section for each task identifies expectations for student responses, ranging from limited understanding to strong understanding.

We describe continuum of student work samples as "Limited Evidence, Adequate Evidence, Strong Evidence" or "Not Yet Started/Ready, Beginning, On Target, Going Beyond." We also present various means by which to examine the student solutions. For example, throughout the book the reader will find samples of checklists, rubrics, and formats for anecdotal records. Each suggested tool is specific to a particular task, although the information could be used in various formats. Again, teachers are the best judge of which means is most effective for their needs and use. The "Looking for Evidence of Understanding" section provides samples of students' work that were examined using the continuum-of-understanding assessment tool and chosen to represent a range of student work across the continuum. The student work samples can guide teachers in looking closely at the work generated by their own students. The final section, "Variations for the Range of Learner," presents ideas for modifying the task to reach more students at both ends of the spectrum as well as ideas for using the task with younger or older students.

In using the suggested variations, the teacher should ensure that the mathematics content does not change in a way that changes the focus of the mathematics being assessed. Each task can be altered by changing the context, breaking the task into subparts, limiting the scope or complexity of the task, or extending the task to offer more challenge or enhance the depth of understanding being assessed.

1

Number and Operations

ENVISION the four-year-old who is just beginning to connect number words with quantities, and compare him or her with the seven-year-old who can reason through multidigit computations using mental strategies. Students grow tremendously in their knowledge of number and operations in the years from prekindergarten through second grade. Across those formative years, the foundation for students' formal mathematical learning is established.

One of the most important accomplishments for young students is the development of number sense, or the ability to use numbers flexibly, meaningfully, and confidently. Number sense develops as students start to understand numbers, ways of representing numbers, and, most important, relationships among numbers. The meanings students establish for small numbers will build a strong conceptual base for subsequent work with place value, larger numbers, and the operations of addition, subtraction, multiplication, and division. Students begin by learning the correct number sequence and acquiring methods for accurately counting sets of objects. Their understanding of numbers takes on new meaning when they connect counting with an understanding of quantity, or *cardinality*. Students make a major leap when they can see and think groups of twos and threes. This ability is the basis for developing part-whole ideas for small numbers, which is eventually extended to larger numbers in which parts can be ten, hundred, or thousand, leading to an understanding of place value and the structure of the base-ten number system.

Students' everyday experiences in solving problems that involve combining and separating objects become formalized during the early elementary school years as addition and subtraction. Students acquire various meanings of addition and subtraction of whole numbers and come to understand the relationship between those two operations. For example, students gain experience with subtraction concepts in take-away, comparison, and missing addend situations. Students also have everyday experiences in solving problems that involve making equal groupings of objects and sharing equally. Such experiences form the basis for understanding multiplication and division.

Students develop computation strategies during the years from prekindergarten to second grade. The range of computational strategies progresses from direct modeling strategies to counting strategies to sophisticated numerical reasoning strategies. When combining seven pencils and five pencils, young students may need to represent both quantities with objects. After representing both sets, they may count all the objects starting at 1. As students gain experience combining sets, they become able to start at 7 and count on the other pencils, "eight, nine, ten, eleven, twelve." When students are able to decompose numbers into small quantities and reason with relationships between numbers, they are ready to move into using numerical reasoning to solve problems. For example, a student may reason, "I can break the five pencils into a group of three pencils and a group of two pencils. Then I can add 7 and 3 to get 10, and then two more pencils gives me 10 plus 2, which equals 12, for a total of twelve pencils."

The assessment tasks in this chapter have been designed and selected for their alignment with the NCTM (2000) Number and Operation Standards and Expectations for prekindergarten through second grade. Our hope is that these tasks open a window to young students' knowledge of number and operations and foster teachers' insights into the thinking and reasoning of their students. As with any assessment, teachers need to think about why they select a particular task, how it might need to be adjusted for their students, and how they are going to use the information to monitor and further support the development of students' mathematical knowledge.

Number and Operations Assessment Items

Standard: Understand numbers, ways of representing numbers, relationships among numbers, and number systems

Expectations

- Count with understanding and recognize "how many" in sets of objects
- Develop understanding of the relative magnitude of whole numbers
- Connect number words and numerals to the quantities they represent

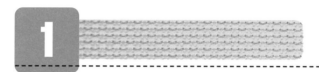

Seven Objects

Grade range: Pre-K–1

About the mathematics: Students' number sense develops as they develop understanding of the size of numbers. The "Seven Objects" task gives teachers insight into students' understanding of quantity and the magnitude of numbers, specifically that of the selected target number. The task requires students to have a sense of how many things "seven" represents. Students are asked to provide non-examples and to discuss the strategies they used for making their selections.

TASK

I was counting objects in our classroom. I counted exactly 7 of the same thing.

What objects in our classroom might I have been counting? Tell me why you picked those objects.

What are some objects in our classroom that couldn't be the ones I counted? Why couldn't they be those objects?

Using this assessment task: This task is designed for use with individual students, thus allowing the teacher to ask probing questions to determine how the child is reasoning about his or her choice. The teacher will need to identify a target number appropriate for the child. The target number should be based on an exact counting of an object in the classroom. For example, exactly seven tables, or seven baskets, may be present in the classroom. The intent of the task is not for the child to guess what object the teacher counted but rather, to identify a set of objects that has the same quantity. Asking the student to explain why he or she selected a particular set of objects not only lends insight into the student's thinking but also introduces and models the concept of justifying one's answer. Asking the student to explain why some objects would not be reasonable choices leads to further insight into the student's reasoning and sense of number magnitude.

Solution: An appropriate solution would identify or describe any set of exactly seven like items that can be found in the classroom setting. In many classrooms, seven windows or seven tables may be an appropriate response, whereas seven pencils or seven people may not be reasonable. A response that is out of context, such as seven lions, would also be unreasonable.

Continuum of Understanding

Limited Understanding
- States a solution that far exceeds 7 or could not possibly be 7
- Interprets the problem as if asked to rote count to 7

Developing Understanding
- Offers a solution that is fairly close to the total quantity of 7 and provides a reasonable explanation for the selection
- Identifies or describes seven random, unlike items found in the classroom, or a subset of a larger group of the same items, such as chairs
- Recognizes a group of seven objects, for example, may state, "I have seven fish," but is unaware that the task asks for items in the classroom

Complete Understanding
- Correctly identifies an object in the classroom that can be counted exactly seven times and provides a sound explanation for the selection
- Recognizes the possibility of multiple correct solutions
- Recognizes a possible answer as too many or too few; for example, may state, "It can't be the blocks, because if I counted all the blocks, it would be a lot more than seven."

Looking for Evidence of Understanding

Susan: Limited Understanding

Susan almost immediately said "children." She explained that a lot of children are in the classroom and that seven is a lot.

Ronaldo: Developing Understanding

Ronaldo also selected "children" and explained that he had counted seven children. When the teacher asked him whether he should also count the other children in the classroom, he said he didn't need to, because he had already counted seven of them. Ronaldo interpreted the task as asking about at least seven objects, not exactly seven. All of his non-examples were quantities smaller than seven, such as one teacher or two sinks.

Maurice: Complete Understanding

After the problem was posed, Maurice quietly looked around the classroom. Then he said, "It could be posters because I counted seven of them on the wall, or it might be pine cones because I think I see seven on the science table." He went on to say, "There are seven projects hanging up because not all people have finished them yet." Maurice had a clear understanding that multiple solutions were possible, and he had a sense of seven as a quantity. He easily provided non-examples, such as chairs, books, people, and crayons. He also commented, "It couldn't be days on the calendar, because there are thirty or thirty-one days in a month."

Variations for the Range of Learners

- The task can be made less or more challenging by decreasing or increasing the target number, depending on the situation and the child. For example, if the class has fifteen students, the problem would be more accessible to some students by using 15 as the target number. For very young children, using a smaller target number, such as 2 or 4, might be more appropriate.
- The setting "in our classroom" can be changed to be less restrictive. Omitting the specific setting may make some solutions, such a number of siblings or pets, more accessible for some students.

Standard: Understand numbers, ways of representing numbers, relationships among numbers, and number systems

Expectations

- Count with understanding
- Demonstrate understanding of the cardinality of numbers
- Demonstrate understanding of the relative magnitude of whole numbers
- Connect number words with the quantities they represent using physical models

Bears in the Box

Grade range: Pre-K–1

About the mathematics: The "Bears in the Box" task lends insight into students' understanding of counting, cardinality of numbers, and magnitude of numbers. Specifically, it requires students first to estimate the number of objects in a set of about twenty objects and then to count the objects. A student's realization that the last counting word tells "how many" indicates an understanding of the cardinality of the set. Next the task presents an opportunity to assess a student's ability to compare the relative magnitude of numbers.

TASK

Fill a small box with bear counters all the way to the top. The box should hold at least twenty bears. Show the open, filled box to the student, and then pose the following questions:

(a) How many bears do you think are in the box?
(b) Next count the bears to find out how many are in the box.
(c) How many bears are in the box?
(d) Is that number more bears or fewer bears than you predicted?

Source: Adapted from *Early Numeracy Interview Booklet* by Department of Education, Employment, and Training (Melbourne, Victoria, Australia: State Government Victoria, 2001).

Using this assessment task: If bear counters are not available, use other small countable objects, such as cubes, and adjust the questions accordingly. The container should be filled to the top with at least twenty counters. A small cup can be used in place of the box. This task is most effectively used with individual students. It can be administered in small groups, but some students are likely to base their predictions on the responses of other students rather than their own reasoning. If you are working with a small group, emphasize to the students that they should think about the amount in their heads and not say a word out loud. Ask each student to very quietly whisper the prediction to the teacher who will record it.

Solution: The solution will vary from student to student. A complete solution should include evidence that a student can count the objects correctly and determine whether his or her estimate is more than or fewer than the actual count. A wide range of responses should be considered reasonable for the estimate. The teacher will need to determine the reasonableness of the estimate on the basis of the objects and container. For example, if five bears can be seen on the top layer, then that number would not be a reasonable estimate, because the student should realize that more bears lie below that layer. However, if the box contains twenty bears, a reasonable estimate may be in the range from ten to thirty.

Continuum of Understanding

Beginning Understanding

- Counts incorrectly (e.g., skips objects, double counts objects, uses an incorrect counting sequence)
- Does not demonstrate an understanding of the cardinality of the set of objects
- Guesses an amount far greater or far less than the actual amount
- Is unable to compare the amounts

Developing Understanding

- Makes minor counting errors, but demonstrates cardinality
- Accurately compares the estimate with the amount counted

Complete Understanding

- Counts correctly, and demonstrates cardinality
- Makes a reasonable estimate
- Accurately compares estimate with the number of objects

Looking for Evidence of Understanding

Aidan: Beginning Understanding

For a box that held twenty-three bears, Aidan, a four-year-old, predicted "hundred" because it is a big number and the quantity in the box looked like a lot of bears. As he counted, he stated a correct number sequence to twelve but then counted "three-teen, five-teen, sixteen, and seventeen." He stopped counting at seventeen because he had lost track of the bears he had counted and those yet to be counted. When the teacher asked him how many bears were in the box, he answered "Hundred" and added, "but I can't count that far." Aidan had acquired a beginning understanding of counting but did not demonstrate cardinality or a sense of the magnitude of numbers.

Victor: Developing Understanding

Victor, a five-year-old, predicted forty-four bears. Victor counted the bears by ones and attempted to keep track of the objects. After he lost track of the bears he had already counted, he asked if he could start over. After he started over for the third time, he counted all the bears but skipped "fifteen" in his word sequence. When he was finished, he said that his final count was twenty-two and that it was close to his guess but smaller.

Mayme: Complete Understanding

Mayme, a six-year-old, first predicted "fifteen" but then changed her response to "12 bears." Then she poured the bears from the box onto the table and began counting by twos. She carefully separated the bears that she had counted from those that she had not yet counted. When she reached twelve, she laughed and immediately acknowledged that her prediction had been too low. She accurately counted twenty-three bears in the box. The teacher asked whether she could figure out how many more bears were in the box than her prediction. Mayme counted out twelve bears by twos and put them to one side. Then she counted the remaining bears by twos. She said and wrote, "11 more bears than I thought."

Variations for the Range of Learners

For those students who have limited experience counting and quantifying sets of objects, the teacher may choose to use fewer objects. More experienced students may be challenged by using a greater number of objects and by being asked to determine the difference between their estimate and the actual number of objects.

Standard: Understand numbers, ways of representing numbers, relationships among numbers, and number systems

Expectations

- Recognize "how many" in sets of objects
- Demonstrate understanding of the relative magnitude of whole numbers
- Connect number words with the quantities they represent, using various physical models and representations

3

Dot Plates

Grade range: Pre-K–1

About the mathematics: *Subitizing* is the ability to quickly "see" a collection of items and to label it with a number. That ability sets the stage for seeing and working with groups of objects rather than individual items. It also takes students beyond counting to considering relationships between and among numbers. The "Dot Plates" task gives the teacher a way to assess students' ability to recognize small sets of objects (e. g., to see twos and threes) in patterned arrangements and tell how many objects are present without counting.

TASK

Prepare a set of dot plates as shown here.

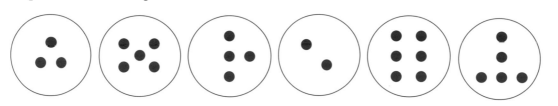

(a) I'm going to show you a dot plate very quickly. I want you to think about the pattern of dots that you see. (Show the pattern for about two seconds, and then turn it over and hide it.)

(b) How many dots did you see?

(c) Describe how you saw the dots?

Repeat the process for the other dot plates.

Using this assessment task: To make a set of dot plates, place dot stickers or draw dots in the patterns shown on white paper plates. For older students or for students with more experience working with quantities, additional dot plates in patterns that range from five to ten dots can be included. The dot arrangements should consist of patterns commonly found on dice or dominos as well as some novel patterns. Ensure that the dots are arranged in recognizable groupings that reveal students' abilities to see groups of twos and threes embedded in the patterns having more dots. This task is designed for use with individual students, allowing the teacher to ask probing questions to determine how the student saw the dots. Watch the students' eyes to determine whether they are counting by ones or whether they appear to recognize groups of twos and threes. Prompt the students to describe how the dots are arranged on each plate.

Solution: The correct solution is the quantity of dots on each plate. Students' explanations will vary but should include evidence to indicate whether the student is counting by ones or is reasoning with groups of two and groups of three.

Continuum of Understanding

Initial Reasoning

May "see" the collection of two dots and perhaps the collection of three dots but still want to count by ones to check

Must count the other dot patterns by ones to determine the total amount

Developing Reasoning

Quickly and confidently sees and labels the collections of two and three dots

Recognizes the common dice or domino pattern for five dots, may recognize the common pattern for six dots, but needs to count the novel patterns by ones

Strong Reasoning

Quickly "sees" and labels the common patterned collections of up to six items with the correct number, and explains how the pattern is composed of twos and threes

Quickly determines the total in the novel patterns by reasoning with groups of twos and threes (e.g., "I saw two and two more, and that is four.")

Looking for Evidence of Understanding

Tracey: Initial Reasoning

Tracey tried to count by ones for each dot pattern. For the patterns with several dots, she often said, "I didn't have time to count it all." For the plate with two dots, she said, "Two" but then added, "I think it was two." Tracey counted by ones for the plate with three dots.

Chase: Developing Reasoning

Chase quickly recognized the quantities on the plates with two, three, and five dots. For the plate with six dots, he said, "Three and three" but did not know the total number of dots unless he counted by ones. For each of the novel patterns, he replied, "I don't know that one" and said he would need to count it to find the answer.

Logan: Strong Reasoning

Logan was able to quickly recognize or determine the total number of dots on all the plates. For two, three, and five, he said, "I just knew it as soon as I saw it." For six, he said, "Three and three is six." For the novel pattern with five dots, he said, "There's three on the bottom, two are going up, and that makes five."

Variations for the Range of Learners

To increase the challenge of the task, make some dot plates that have more-complex patterns, such as those shown below, or show two plates at a time. To lessen the challenge, limit the arrangements of dots to the familiar patterns found on dice and double-six dominoes.

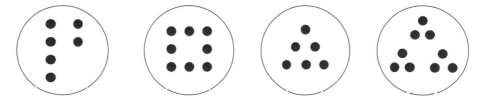

Standards
- Understand numbers, ways of representing numbers, relationships among numbers, and number systems
- Understand meanings of operations and how they relate to one another
- Compute fluently and make reasonable estimates

Expectations
- Develop a sense of whole numbers and represent and use them in flexible ways, including relating, composing, and decomposing numbers
- Understand various meanings of addition and subtraction of whole numbers and the relationship between the two operations
- Develop and use strategies for whole-number computations, with a focus on addition
- Use variety of methods and tools to compute, including objects, mental computation, and paper and pencil
- Create and use representations to organize, record, and communicate mathematical ideas

How Many of Each

Grade range: K–2

About the mathematics: The "How Many of Each" task reveals students' understanding of part-part-whole relationships. Thinking about a number in terms of its parts is an important milestone in the development of early number sense. Part-part-whole relationships are also an important bridge to addition, subtraction, and fraction concepts. This task requires that students use strategies for generating, recording, and organizing part-part combinations for the whole number 8. Students with less experience will generate possibilities through trial and error, whereas students with more experience will begin to notice patterns and relationships. The commutative property is inherent in the problem, and possible combinations can be thought of in pairs, for example, $1 + 7$ and $7 + 1$.

> **TASK**
>
> Some apples and some bananas are on a tray. There are 8 pieces of fruit in all.
>
> (a) How many apples and how many bananas could be on the tray?
> (b) Is another solution possible?
>
> Record your answers on paper using pictures, numbers, or words.

Using this assessment task: This problem can be presented to the whole class. Each student should have counters in two different colors along with paper and colored pencils or crayons. The teacher circulates around the room, and may need to prompt some students to generate more than one solution and to remind them that exactly eight pieces of fruit are present in all. Most students will likely use a trial-and-error approach to generate solutions, but some students may begin to recognize patterns within the combinations. Students will demonstrate a range of representations, from concrete and pictorial images to abstract notation and addition sentences.

Solution: Students may choose to show the combinations with pictures, words, symbols, or equations. The problem has seven possible solutions:

1 apple, 7 bananas (1 + 7 = 8)
2 apples, 6 bananas (2 + 6 = 8)
3 apples, 5 bananas (3 + 5 = 8)
4 apples, 4 bananas (4 + 4 = 8)
5 apples, 3 bananas (5 + 3 = 8)
6 apples, 2 bananas (6 + 2 = 8)
7 apples, 1 banana (7 + 1 = 8)

The task states that "some apples and some bananas" are present; therefore, the combinations of 0 apples and 8 bananas and 8 apples and 0 bananas would typically be excluded. If students include those possibilities, however, their reasoning may demonstrate a strong understanding of the concept rather than a lack of understanding.

Continuum of Understanding

Levels 1 and 2: Needs More Experience

1: Does not understand the problem and/or does not record any correct combinations of 8

2: Finds and records one combination of 8 with assistance

Levels 3 and 4: Beginning

3: Records one combination of 8 unassisted

4: Records one combination of 8 and is able to find at least one other combination with assistance

Levels 5 and 6: Developing

5: Records two combinations of 8 unassisted

6: Records more than two combinations through extensive trial and error

Levels 7 and 8: Strong

7: Records most of the combinations of 8 and is aware of a pattern that is emerging

8: Generates, organizes, and records results systematically

Looking for Evidence of Understanding

Dylan: Beginning Level 3

In this problem, many students started with the combination of four apples and four bananas before generating other possibilities. Dylan quickly and confidently found and recorded the combination of 4 apples and 4 bananas without using counters. At that point he was satisfied with his answer, even after being prompted to find another possibility.

Kaden: Developing Level 5

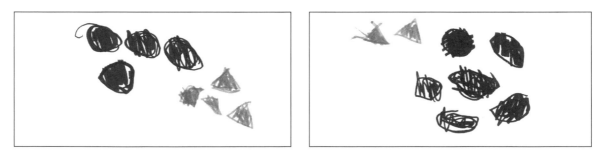

Kaden also recorded four apples and four bananas immediately. When the teacher prompted him to try to find another possibility, he used his counters and found the combination of two bananas and six apples through trial and error.

Gabby: Developing Level 6

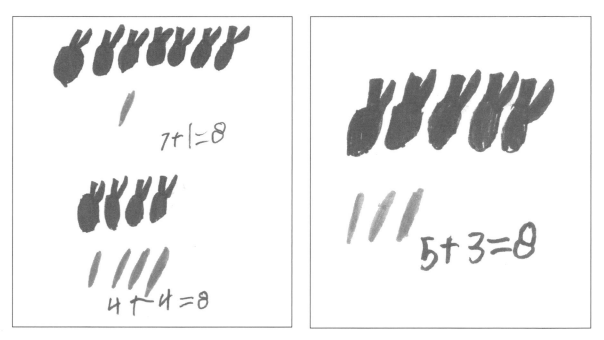

Gabby generated and recorded two possibilities very quickly and recorded them as pictures and as addition sentences, 7 + 1 = 8 and 4 + 4 = 8. She tried for several more minutes to find a third combination but often reported too many pieces of fruit (e.g., five apples and four bananas) until she proudly announced that she had found another one, five apples and three bananas.

Rebecca: Strong Level 8

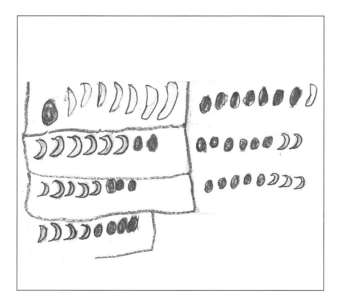

Rebecca systematically recorded 1 apple and 7 bananas and then recorded 7 apples and 1 banana. Next she recorded 2 apples and 6 bananas and then 6 apples and 2 bananas. She continued systematically drawing the pairs until she had seven possible combinations. She asked, "Can I include eight apples and zero bananas and zero and eight?" The teacher responded, "Do what you think answers the problem the best." Rebecca decided not to include those two combinations.

Variations for the Range of Learners

- The task can be made more or less challenging by increasing or decreasing the target number.
- The problem can be made more difficult by adding another type of fruit, such as using oranges, apples, and bananas. The solutions will then require three parts.

Standards
- Understand numbers, ways of representing numbers, relationships among numbers, and number systems
- Understand meanings of operations and how they relate to one another
- Compute fluently and make reasonable estimates

Expectations
- Develop a sense of whole numbers and represent and use them in flexible ways, including relating, composing, and decomposing numbers
- Understand the effects of adding and subtracting whole numbers
- Develop and use strategies for whole-number computations
- Communicate mathematical thinking coherently and clearly to others
- Select and use various types of reasoning

5

Comparing Pairs

Grade range: K–2

About the mathematics: The "Comparing Pairs" task assesses students' understanding of the concepts "more," "less," and the "same," as well their understanding of number relationships and the operation of addition. In "Comparing Pairs," students play with a partner. Each student is given two number cards and asked to state whether the sum of their two numbers is more than, less than, or the same as their partner's. Students may be successful at this task by using a variety of strategies including counting, using number relationships between sets, or estimating mentally and adding.

TASK

Using the set of number cards from 0 to 9, give each person two cards.

Prompt: Look at each pair of numbers.

(a) Who has more?

(b) Who has less?

(c) Are the sums the same?

Explain your reasoning.

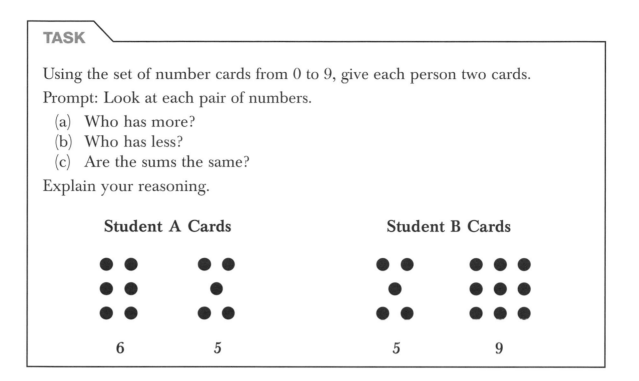

Student A Cards

6   5

Student B Cards

5   9

Using this assessment task: Although students may engage in this task in pairs, to assess their understanding of the concepts, the teacher should require that the students individually explain their reasoning or provide written explanations. For example, one teacher allowed her students to play in pairs but interrupted their games to play with individual students using three sets of predetermined cards including (6, 5) and (5, 9); (6, 8) and (7, 9); and (6, 7) and (8, 5). Each pair of students will need a deck of twenty number cards. Copy and cut apart the "Number Cards" blackline masters. Note that the patterns on sheet 1 and sheet 2 vary to give students more options for comparing the numbers. The dot patterns on the number cards allow alternative strategies for making comparisons, such as counting on or using visual number relationships. Although proper use of mathematical language is not explicitly assessed in this task, encourage students to use the language of *more, less, same* or *greater than, less than, equal to* rather than the words *bigger* or *smaller*. Young students' experiences with the concept of "less than" are often minimal, so ensure that students frequently identify who has "less," not only who has "more."

Solution: The focus of this task is on identifying quantities as more, less, and the same, not on calculating sums. Although determining the sums is one strategy, other acceptable approaches can be used. For example, if Student A has cards showing 6 and 5 and Student B has cards showing 5 and 9, here are three possible solution strategies:

Strategy 1: Adding
6 + 5 = 11
5 + 9 = 14
Student A has less; student B has more.

Strategy 2: Comparing numbers in the sets
Both sets have a 5. Since 6 is less than 9, Student A has less.

Strategy 3: Using benchmarks to estimate
6 and 5 is close to 10.
5 and 9 is a lot more than 10, so Student B has more.

Continuum of Understanding

Unjustified or Unreasonable

- Is not able to consistently identify *more, less,* or *same* correctly
- Uses inappropriate strategies to compare sums
- Is unable to communicate ideas or understanding

Partially Justified

- Is able to identify *more, less,* or *same* correctly most of the time
- Uses strategies that do not always lead to a successful solution or may be inefficient
- Uses limited reasoning or does not express it clearly

Fully Justified

- Consistently identifies *more, less,* or *same* correctly
- Employs a strategy that incorporates the use of number relationships to compare sums efficiently
- Effectively communicates a clear and reasonable explanation

Looking for Evidence of Understanding

For this task, the teacher interrupted pairs to assess individual students using predetermined sets of cards. The student was given pattern cards for 6 and 5 and asked to compare them with the teacher's cards of 5 and 9.

Jackson: Unjustified or Unreasonable

As Jackson looked at the two sets of number cards, he asked whether he could count them. The teacher nodded. He counted the dots on each card and incorrectly counted ten for his cards (6, 5) and correctly counted fourteen for the teacher cards (5, 9). When given the second set of cards, Jackson used the same counting strategy. He did not attempt to answer the question of who had more and who had less unless prompted. Although he occasionally answered correctly, whether he was basing his answer on the sums he had counted was not clear.

Ravi: Partially Justified

The teacher asked Ravi who had less, the student (6, 5) or the teacher (5, 9). He hesitated and then answered, "You have more than me."
Teacher: "How do you know that?"
Ravi: "Because you have lots," and pointed to the dots on the number cards.
Teacher: "How can you be sure?"
Ravi: "Look! You have lots more than me."
Although Ravi is convinced he is correct here, his strategy of using a visual estimation was less successful when the difference in the sums was small.

Lillian: Fully Justified

Lillian explained, "It's simple!" and indicated that the pair (5, 9) was greater. "It's like 5 plus 5 is 10 and then you need, I think, 4 more. If you compare 6 and 9, they don't match but 5 and 5 do match. Nine is more than 5, and 5 is not more than 5, so 9 and 5 is the most." Lillian looked for number relationships across the sets of cards in subsequent sets. When she was not able to see a relationship, she altered her strategy and added the sums to make a comparison.

Variations for the Range of Learners

- Limit the size of the numbers for less experienced students. You may choose to include number cards from 0 to 5 only or to eliminate the need for comparing sums by giving only one card to each person.
- Increase the difficulty of the task by including number cards from 0 to 20 (with or without dots), by dealing three number cards to each person, or by having students play in groups of three to compare three sets of sums.

Standards
- Understand meanings of operations and how they relate to one another
- Compute fluently and make reasonable estimates

Expectations
- Understand various meanings of addition and subtraction of whole numbers and the relationship between the two operations
- Create and use representations to organize, record, and communicate mathematical ideas
- Develop and use strategies for whole-number computations

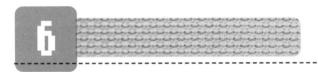

Bracelets

Grade range: K–2

About the mathematics: Students' early encounters with addition and subtraction story problems usually involve "joining" and "separating" (i.e., take-away) situations. Students develop further understandings of those operations when they solve missing-addend problems that arise from stories or real situations. Such types of situations also help students see the relationship between addition and subtraction. The "Bracelets" task fosters insights into students' understanding of missing-addend story problems, which are sometimes referred to as "join change-unknown" word problems.

TASK

Lisa is making bracelets. She has already made 8 bracelets.

She needs to make 12 all together so she can give one to each of her cousins.

How many more bracelets does she need to make?

Show how you solved this problem. Use pictures, numbers, and words.

Using this assessment task: This task can be presented to the whole class. Write the "Bracelet" story problem on the board or overhead projector. Provide students with blank paper and colored pencils or crayons. Have connecting cubes or counters accessible so that students may use them if they choose. Pose the story problem to the students. Tell the students that they may use cubes or other materials to figure out the solution to the story problem. Each student should represent his or her solution strategy and the solution to the problem on the paper (for example, by using pictures, words, and numbers). If students do not produce a number sentence, prompt them to write a number sentence that matches the story.

Solution: The solution to the problem is "4 more bracelets." A student may be able to figure out a solution to the problem and to explain how he or she obtained the solution but may struggle with writing an accurate equation. Any equation that shows the relationship among the quantities would be acceptable, for example, "8 + 4 = 12" or "12 − 8 = 4."

Continuum of Understanding

Limited Understanding

* Answers with the number that is more (i.e., 12), or adds the two numbers
* Draws a picture of the two quantities but does not show a solution, for example, draws 8 bracelets and draws 12 cousins

Developing Understanding

* Uses appropriate reasoning and representation but makes computational errors
* Arrives at the correct solution but cannot explain his or her reasoning nor draw a picture that shows the situation or identifies the solution
* Writes an incorrect number sentence

Strong Understanding

* Demonstrates reasoning when using direct modeling, counting on (e.g., starts at 8, and counts on: 9, 10, 11, 12), or numerical reasoning (e.g., indicates that 2 bracelets are needed to get to 10, and 2 more are needed to get to 12, so 4 bracelets are needed) to solve the problem
* Produces a representation that clearly identifies the answer as "4 bracelets"
* Writes an accurate number sentence that illustrates the relationship among the quantities

Looking for Evidence of Understanding

Pamela: Limited Understanding

> She is bone with 8 bracelets. She needs to make 12 morehow many Does that make 21

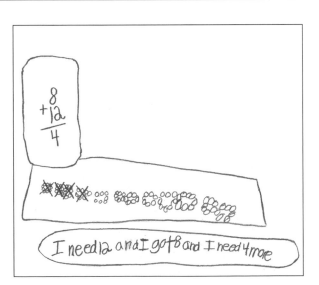

Several students in the first grade class did not understand the question that was being asked and just added the numbers. Pamela explained that the problem said Lisa needed to make "more," so that means you have to add the two numbers together. She drew eight bracelets and then drew twelve more bracelets. Her picture has a total of twenty bracelets, but Pamela double counted one bracelet and thought that the total number of bracelets was twenty-one.

Isabel: Developing Understanding

Isabel demonstrated an understanding of the situation. She clearly drew twelve bracelets, counted out eight of them, and figured four more were needed, as shown by the crossed-off bracelets. However, her number sentence is incorrect. She knew that four bracelets was the answer, so she thought that the 4 had to be in the "answer spot." Most of the students in this first-grade class were at the "developing" level—they could figure out the answer but were not sure how to write an appropriate number sentence.

$$\begin{array}{r} 8 \\ +12 \\ \hline 4 \end{array}$$

I need 12 and I got 8 and I need 4 more

Denice: Strong Understanding

Denice did not need to represent all twelve bracelets. She explained that she knew Lisa had eight bracelets, so she just counted on, "nine, ten, eleven, twelve," and used her fingers to keep track of the counts. Then she drew a picture of the eight bracelets Lisa had and wrote "4 to get to 12." Denice also was able to explain how her number sentence related to the story.

Variation for the Range of Learners

- For students who have limited experience with such types of situations, the teacher may want to have the students act out the situation in the whole-class grouping. One student can pretend to be Lisa, who has eight bracelets, and twelve other students can be the cousins. Stop once the situation is clear in the students' minds, and ask them to represent the situation on their paper and to solve the problem on their own.
- The task can be made more or less challenging by increasing or decreasing the size of the numbers in the story problem.

Standards
- Understand numbers, ways of representing numbers, relationships among numbers, and number systems
- Understand meanings of operations and how they relate to one another
- Compute fluently and make reasonable estimates

Expectations
- Compare and contrast the properties of numbers and number systems, including the rational and real numbers
- Use multiple models to develop initial understandings of place value and the base-ten number system
- Understand various meanings of addition and subtraction of whole numbers
- Develop and use strategies for whole-number computation
- Use a variety of methods and tools to compute, including objects, mental computation, estimation, and paper and pencil
- Apply and adapt a variety of appropriate strategies to solve problems
- Communicate mathematical thinking coherently and clearly to peers, teachers, and others
- Use representations to model and interpret mathematical phenomena

How Far Apart

Grade range: 1–2

About the mathematics: Students typically have many experiences with "take away" subtraction problems but often have difficulty with less familiar subtraction situations involving comparisons or "difference." In the "How Far Apart" task, students are asked to solve a subtraction problem situated in a measurement or distance context: How far apart are two given seats in an auditorium? Students may use a variety of strategies and representations to demonstrate their understanding of difference, from direct modeling and counting to invented or standard algorithms.

TASK

Jaimie and Kendra both had tickets to the play. Jaimie had seat number 25, and Kendra had seat number 37. Both seats are in the same row.

How far apart are the seats? Explain your reasoning.

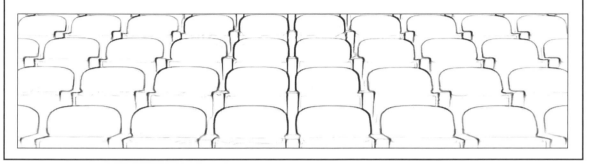

Using this assessment task: This task can be done with the whole class. Present the problem to students, and address any questions about the context. Students will need paper, a pencil, and a variety of tools to help them generate solutions, for example, counters, number lines or metric rulers, hundred charts, and base-ten blocks. Encourage students to solve the problem in more than one way, perhaps by using different representations.

Solution: The correct solution is 12 seats apart. Students may arrive at the solution using a variety of strategies.

Continuum of Understanding

Limited Understanding

- Does not understand the problem
- Does not have a strategy to determine or describe the difference between 25 and 37, or describes the situation qualitatively, such as, "not very far"

Developing Understanding

- Understands the nature of the problem but may not use a strategy that leads to a correct solution
- May count the number of seats rather than the distance between seats; for example, may count the number of seats between 25 and 37, leading to an incorrect solution of 11, or may count all the seats including 25 and 37, leading to an incorrect solution of 13

On Target

- Uses a strategy to correctly demonstrate the difference between 25 and 37, but the strategy may be inefficient or limited to direct modeling or counting on by ones
- Clearly communicates the selected strategy

Strong Understanding

- Uses a strategy that demonstrates an understanding of place value by using tens and ones, for example, calculates $25 + 10 = 35$, $35 + 2 = 37$, and notes that the difference is $10 + 2$, or 12
- Recognizes the relationship between different representations used to solve this problem

Looking for Evidence of Understanding

Kenny: Developing Understanding

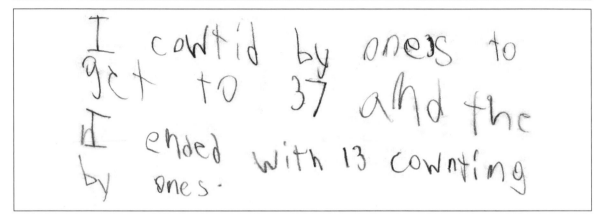

Kenny circled the numbers 25 and 37 on a hundreds chart. Then he counted all the numbers, including 25, to arrive at a solution of 13. On his paper Kenny wrote, "I counted by ones to get to 37 and then I ended with 13 counting by ones."

Leia: On Target

Leia correctly used a counting on strategy. She started at 25 and counted the number of "jumps" between 25 and 37 to determine the correct difference.

Mason: Strong Understanding

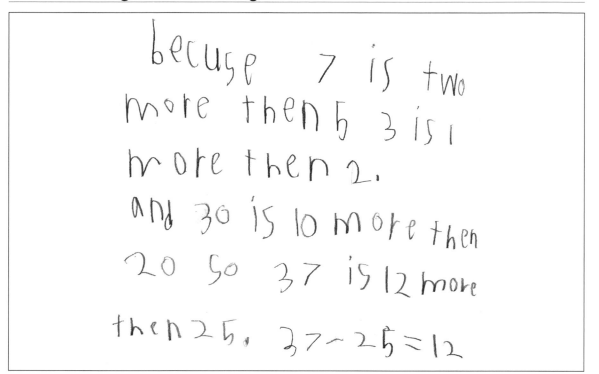

becuse 7 is two
more then 5 3 is 1
more then 2.
and 30 is 10 more then
20 So 37 is 12 more
then 25. 37-25=12

Mason used his understanding of tens and ones to solve this problem. First he compared the ones and said that "7 is two more than 5." Next he compared the tens. Although he stated that "3 is one more than 2," he used that fact as a bridge to the next statement, "and 30 is 10 more than 20." Mason also recognized the situation as a subtraction problem and included the equation: $37 - 25 = 12$.

Variations for the Range of Learners

Make the problem more or less difficult by choosing different seat numbers. For example, less experienced students may solve the problem using seat numbers 8 and 13, whereas more experienced students may solve it using 58 and 73.

Standard: Understand meanings of operations and how they relate to one another

Expectations

- Understand various meanings of subtraction of whole numbers and the relationship between addition and subtraction
- Understand the effects of subtracting whole numbers
- Monitor and reflect on the process of mathematical problem solving

8

What's the Story?

Grade range: 1–2

About the mathematics: The "What's the Story?" task offers insights into students' understanding of the meanings of operations and of the relationship between addition and subtraction. Specifically, it focuses on students' understanding of subtracting whole numbers. It asks students to describe a subtraction situation for a given expression.

TASK

Michael's teacher read a story problem. Michael wrote down the number sentence

$$15 - 9 = \square$$

to match the problem that was in the story. What could the story problem have been?

Using this assessment task: This task can be used with the whole class. The teacher can write the number sentence on the board and then pose the prompt to the students. Give students paper and pencils for writing out their story problems. As the students work, the teacher can individually ask any student who needs writing support to dictate his or her story problem, then record the response on the student's paper. The teacher may also want to probe the thinking of some students by asking, "How does your story relate to the number sentence written on the board?"

Solution: The solutions suggested will vary from student to student. A complete solution will include evidence that a student can successfully pose a story problem that involves finding the difference between 15 and 9. The story problem may involve separating, comparison, or missing-addend situations; for example: "Luis had 15 cookies. He ate 9 of them. How many cookies does he have now?" "James has 15 markers and Kendra has 9 markers. How many more markers does James have?" "Rochelle has $9. She needs $15 to buy the toy. How much more money does she need to earn?"

Continuum of Understanding

Limited Understanding
- Does not understand the request to pose a story problem and just restates the equation and attempts to figure out the answer
- Describes an addition situation that may or may not use the numbers 15 and 9

Developing Understanding
- Describes a subtraction situation that involves the numbers 15 and 9 but either does not ask a question or poses a question that is not appropriate to the situation, for example, may ask, "How many in all?"

Complete Understanding
- Describes a situation that involves finding the difference between 15 and 9 and asks an appropriate question
- Is able to explain how the story problem relates to the number sentence

Looking for Evidence of Understanding

Devin: Limited Understanding

Devin drew fifteen circles on his paper, crossed off nine of them, and then wrote his equation. When the teacher prompted him for the story problem, he just restated the equation with the answer, "Fifteen minus nine equals six."

Gale: Developing Understanding

$15 - 9 = 6$

Ms. cording has 15 apples.

she gave Michael 9. how meny

~~did~~ dose Ms. cordind

have in all?

Gale described a subtraction situation about giving away apples but was not able to formulate an appropriate question. She wrote, "How many does Ms. Cording have in all?" When the teacher prompted her about whether she wrote a correct question, Gale underlined the letter "h" in "how" and said that it was wrong because it should be an uppercase letter. Otherwise she thought her question was fine.

Brendan: Complete Understanding

$15 - 9 =$ I has 15 snow man I gave 9 away now how meny do I have

Almost all the students who wrote an appropriate story problem depicted a separating or "take away" situation and wrote the question "How many are left?" Brendan also wrote a story about giving away some objects, but he phrased his question as "Now how many do I have?" Brendan was able to clearly explain how his story matched the equation and was also able to figure out the answer.

Variations for the Range of Learners

- The task can be made less challenging by using single-digit numbers in the equation, for example, "7 – 5 = 2," or by posing an addition sentence, for example, "8 + 4 = 12."
- The task can be made more challenging by asking students to tell story problems for related equations in which the unknown occurs in different positions in the equation, for example, "15 – □ = 6" or "□ – 9 = 6" or "6 + □ = 15."

Standards
- Understand numbers, ways of representing numbers, relationships among numbers, and number systems
- Understand meanings of operations and how they relate to one another

Expectations
- Develop a sense of whole numbers and represent and use them in flexible ways including relating, composing, and decomposing numbers
- Understand the effects of adding and subtracting two whole numbers
- Create and use representations to organize, record, and communicate mathematical ideas

Secret Numbers

Grade range: 1–2

About the mathematics: The "Secret Numbers" task fosters insight into students' understanding of how to decompose numbers into part-part-whole relationships. It reveals students' understanding of the commutative property and whether they view such pairs as $3 + 5$ and $5 + 3$ as the same combination of numbers. The task also requires students to determine whether combinations satisfy the conditions of the problem.

TASK

I'm thinking of two different numbers. When you add them together, they make 8.

When I asked some people to guess my secret numbers, four people came up with four different answers.

Do you think that it is possible for four different answers all to be correct? Explain your thinking.

Source: Adapted from *Mathematics Assessment: A Practical Handbook for Grades K–2,* by Florence Glanfield, William S. Bush, and Jean Kerr Stenmark (Reston, VA: National Council of Teachers of Mathematics, 2003).

Using this assessment task: This problem can be used with the whole class or with small groups of students. Students should have access to counters or connecting cubes in at least two different colors and be given paper for recording their reasoning. The teacher may have to prompt students to re-examine their solutions in relation to the problem conditions, for example, "What might the two different secret numbers be?" "Can you list four different ways to find the secret numbers?"

Solution: For a complete solution, the student responds, "Yes, it is possible" and provides evidence that he or she can generate the four combinations of 8 that use two different numbers: 1 + 7, 2 + 6, 3 + 5, and 0 + 8.

Continuum of Understanding

Limited Understanding

- May not understand the problem or state that the task is possible but does not give examples of possible solutions; may produce only the answer 4 and 4

Developing Understanding

- Indicates that more than one correct way can be used to solve $a + b = 8$ but is not able to accurately relate the combinations to the second part of the task
- Does not offer all four possibilities, or counts such equations as $3 + 5 = 8$ and $5 + 3 = 8$ as different solutions, or includes $4 + 4$ as one of the solutions

Complete Understanding

- Clearly communicates how two different numbers can make 8 and explains the possibility that four people can get four different solutions
- Also explains why $4 + 4$ does not satisfy one of the problem's conditions, which specifies two *different* numbers

Evidence of Understanding

Ramona: Limited Understanding

Ramona, like several students, responded, "I think it might be possible." When prompted, she was able to provide only $4 + 4$ as an example. Other students said that different solutions were not possible because the only solution they could think of was $4 + 4$.

Dominic: Developing Understanding

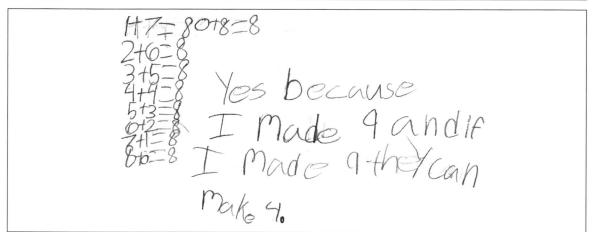

Dominic systematically recorded all the combinations of 8. Next he counted the number of equations and concluded that nine solutions were possible. Dominic did not take into account that 4 + 4 does not meet the conditions of the problem, nor did he consider that such equations as $2 + 6 = 8$ and $6 + 2 = 8$ are the same combination of numbers.

Lenora: Complete Understanding

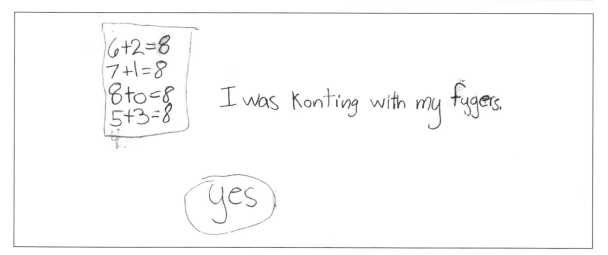

As Lenora began to work on the problem, she commented, "It couldn't be 4 + 4" and explained that the problem said the combination had to be two different numbers. Lenora used her fingers to help her determine the combinations and was careful to check each new combination with those written on her paper to avoid duplicates. For example, when she checked "2 + 6" against her list, she stated, "Got that one." Lenora concluded, "Yes," it is possible for four people to all come up with different correct answers.

x

Variations for the Range of Learners

The task can be made less challenging by using an odd number, such as 7 or 11, for the target number, and adjusting the second part of the problem as needed. This variation removes the extra step in the thinking that is involved with even numbers and the tendency of students to include a double, such as 4 + 4, as a solution. A larger even number can be used to increase the challenge of the problem. Any time a number is changed in the problem, one needs to examine the second part of the problem to determine whether more or fewer possible solutions can be found.

Standards

- Understand numbers, ways of representing numbers, relationships among numbers, and number systems
- Understand meanings of operations and how they relate to one another

Expectations

- Understand and represent commonly used fractions, such as 1/4, 1/3, and 1/2
- Understand situations that entail multiplication and division, such as equal groups of objects and sharing equally

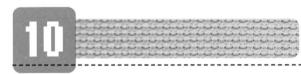

The Photograph

Grade range: 1–2

About the mathematics: In the "Photograph" task, students are asked to imagine a photograph in which half the people are girls and half are boys. The primary assessment focus is to determine students' conceptual understanding of fractional parts of a set. Although most young students will be familiar with the word *half* in informal contexts of sharing, they may not have developed the understanding that fractional parts require equal shares or equal-sized portions. Only the conceptual understanding of one-half is expected in this situation, not the symbolic notation. This task is open-ended, in that the students are asked to choose the size of the whole, or in this instance the number of people in the photograph. The equal groupings and doubling structure of this task also connect it with multiplication and division concepts.

> ### TASK
>
> I'm imagining a photograph of girls and boys at the zoo. Half of the people in the photograph are girls. How many girls and how many boys might be in the photograph?
>
> Draw a picture of what you think the photograph looks like.

Using this assessment task: The task can be posed to the whole class. Supply students with paper and colored pencils or crayons. Such objects as people-shaped counters may help some students get started. The task states that the photograph shows boys and girls and that half of the people are girls. A student with a clear understanding of fractions will realize that if half of the people are girls, the other half must be boys. Students who do not have a clear understanding of fractions may not realize that the number of boys must equal the number of girls in the photograph. As the students are drawing their pictures, ask them how many boys and girls will be in their completed picture.

Solution: An appropriate solution would be a drawing or a physical representation showing an equal number of males and females.

Continuum of Understanding

Limited Understanding
- Draws a picture in which the number of boys and the number of girls in the drawing drawn are unrelated
- When asked about the drawing, does not communicate an understanding of halves being equal

Developing Understanding
- Produces an initial drawing that does not reflect a clear understanding of equal parts; after some prompting, realizes that the halves must be equal

On Target
- Understands that the total number of females must equal the number of males, and produces a drawing that reflects that understanding
- May also realize that an even number of people are needed in the photograph

Looking for Evidence of Understanding

Tina: Limited Understanding

Children who did not understand the idea of half were often sidetracked by the drawing and got lost in the scenario. They asked, "May I draw a cat or a dog?" or claimed that some of the people got eaten by the lion. Tina's picture shows 4 girls and 3 boys. When asked if half of the people in the picture were girls, she named the girls and boys but did not refer to the concept of half.

Selena: Developing Understanding

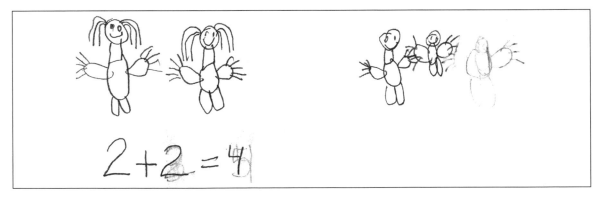

Selena drew her picture with two girls and three boys and wrote an addition sentence at the bottom, $2 + 3 = 5$. The teacher prompted her to think about the question again and said, "Half of the people in the picture are girls and half are boys." Selena said, "Oh yeah, they should be the same." Selena erased one of the boys and changed her addition sentence.

Jeremy: On Target

Jeremy was very careful when drawing his picture. He knew that if half of the people were girls, half would be boys. For every girl he drew, he immediately drew a boy to ensure that he had an equal number of each. He stopped when he had 4 girls and 4 boys. In describing his picture, he pointed to his mom and dad, his two sisters, himself, his cousin Jeffrey, his aunt, and the new baby. When asked how many people are in the picture, he said "Four and four are eight."

Variations for the Range of Learners

*   Asking a question that is less open-ended may be helpful for some students. For example, "Half of the people in the photograph are girls. I see five girls in the picture. How many boys are in the picture? How many people are in the photograph altogether?"
*   Choose fractions other than half, for example, a fourth or a third.
*   The question can be modified by stating that "more than half" or "fewer than half" are female.

Standard: Understand meanings of operations and how they relate to one another

Expectations

- Understand meanings of addition of whole numbers
- Understand situations that entail multiplication and division, such as equal groupings of objects
- Create and use representations to organize, record, and communicate mathematical ideas
- Apply and adapt a variety of appropriate strategies to solve problems

11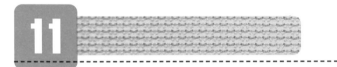

Packages of Gum

Grade range: 1–2

About the mathematics: The "Packages of Gum" task lends insight into students' emerging understanding of the concepts of multiplication and division. Students' are asked to work with a situation that involves repeated joining (addition) of groups of equal size. The task reveals students' understanding of equal-sized groups and their ability to represent such groups in a drawing. Further, students are asked to write a number sentence, with the expectation that they write an addition equation with three addends.

TASK

Robin has 3 packages of gum. Each package has 5 pieces of gum.

How many pieces of gum does Robin have altogether?

Draw a picture to show how much gum Robin has. Find the answer, and write a number sentence to solve the problem.

Using this assessment task: This task can be presented to the whole class. Write the "Packages of Gum" story problem on the chalkboard or overhead projector. Give students blank paper for representing the problem and for recording their solution. Allow students to use cubes or other objects to solve the problem. Pose the problem to the students. Tell the students that they are to draw a picture that shows Robin's gum and then should figure how many pieces of gum she has altogether. If students do not write a number sentence initially, prompt them to write a number sentence that matches the problem.

Solution: The solution to the problem is "15 pieces of gum." The student's picture should clearly show three equal groups with five objects in each group. The expected number sentence that matches the story is "5 + 5 + 5 = 15." If students have experience writing multiplication equations, an acceptable solution would be "$3 \times 5 = 15$" or "$5 \times 3 = 15$." With either multiplication equation, the teacher should ask the student to explain the meaning of each number in the equation (e.g., the 3 tells the number of groups, and the 5 tells how many are in each group).

Continuum of Understanding

Limited Understanding
- Gives an answer of "3" or "5"
- Adds the two numbers and says the answer is 8, or makes a counting error
- Shows either a group of three or a group of five, or both of those groups

Beginning Understanding
- Draws a picture showing three equal groups with five objects in each, but says that the answer is 8
- May write $3 + 5 = 8$

Developing Understanding
- Draws a picture showing three equal groups with five objects in each, and says that the answer is 15
- Writes an incorrect number sentence, such as $3 + 5 = 15$

Strong Understanding
- Draws a picture that clearly shows three equal groups of five objects in each and reveals that the correct answer is 15
- Describes his or her strategy for solving the problem verbally or in writing (e.g., counting by ones or skip counting by fives)
- Writes a correct number sentence, such as $5 + 5 = 5 = 15$

Looking for Evidence of Understanding

Garland: Limited Understanding

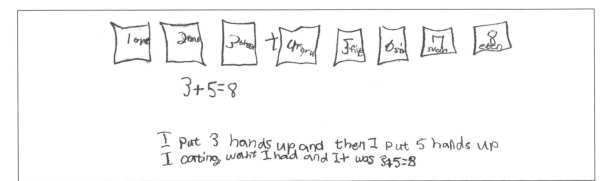

Garland focused on the numbers in the problem rather than the situation. He added the two numbers, and wrote, "I put 3 hands up and then I put 5 hands up. I [was] counting what I had and it was $3 + 5 = 8$." Garland wrote "hands," but he doubtless meant "fingers" because he demonstrated that he put up three fingers and five fingers and counted them all by ones.

Stephen: Beginning Understanding

Stephen drew an appropriate picture that showed three groups of five; however, he wrote $3 + 5 = 8$ as his number sentence. When the teacher asked him how many pieces of gum altogether, he said, "Eight."

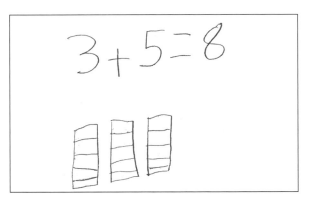

Sabina: Developing Understanding

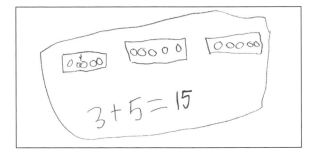

Sabina was able to draw a picture that showed what was happening in the problem. She drew three rectangles and put five pieces of gum in each rectangle. She knew that the total was 15 pieces of gum, but she incorrectly wrote $3 + 5 = 15$ as her number sentence.

Caleb: Strong Understanding

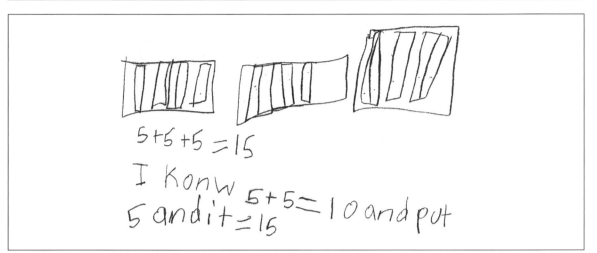

Caleb demonstrated a strong understanding of the gum task. He readily drew a picture that showed three groups with five pieces of gum in each group. He then explained how he skip counted by five to get the answer. He wrote, "I know $5 + 5 = 10$ and put [add another] 5 and it equals 15." He correctly wrote $5 + 5 + 5 = 15$ as his number sentence.

Variations for the Range of Learners

The task can be made more or less challenging by increasing or decreasing the number of objects in each group or the number of groups.

Standard: Understand meanings of operations and how they relate to one another

Expectations

- Understand situations that entail multiplication and division, such as equal groupings of objects and sharing equally
- Create and use representations to organize, record, and communicate mathematical ideas
- Communicate mathematical thinking coherently to others
- Apply and adapt a variety of appropriate strategies to solve problems

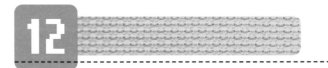

Watching a Movie

Grade range: 1–2

About the mathematics: This task assesses students' understanding of a multiplicative structure in a problem-solving situation. In "Watching a Movie," the whole is known (i.e., the number of people watching the movie), but the number of groups (i.e., rows) and the number in each group (i.e., chairs) are unknown. Students may use repeated addition or their understanding of multiplication and division to determine one or more solutions to the problem. A formal understanding of factors or the relationship between multiplication and division is not expected; instead, the task assesses students' informal understanding of equal-sized groups.

TASK

Twelve people are going to watch a movie. The movie theater has 12 chairs. Each row has the same number of chairs. How many rows does the theater have?

Draw a picture of your solution.

Are any other answers possible? How do you know?

Using this assessment task: The "Watching a Movie" task can be done with the whole class. The teacher should discuss the problem with the students and relate the problem to their experiences of sitting in rows in a movie theatre, at school, and at sporting events. Students will need twelve tiles or counters and paper, and some students may also want to use colored pencils or crayons. Encourage students to test their ideas with the counters. The teacher may have to remind some students of the constraint—that the same number of chairs are in each row. Once students have generated and drawn a solution, prompt them to look for another answer.

Solution: This problem has six solutions:

   a. 1 row with 12 chairs (1 × 12)

   b. 12 rows with 1 chair in each (12 × 1)

   c. 2 rows with 6 chairs in each (2 × 6)

   d. 6 rows with 2 chairs in each (6 × 2)

   e. 3 rows with 4 chairs in each (3 × 4)

   f. 4 rows with 3 chairs in each (4 × 3)

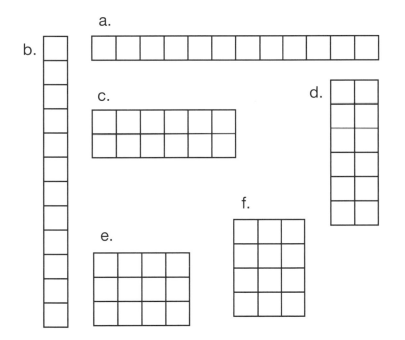

Continuum of Understanding

Questions	High Level	Moderate Level	Low Level
Does the student communicate the solution clearly?	Yes, the student uses a clear representation or equations to demonstrate understanding.	The solution requires some interpretation or clarification by the student.	No, the representation is unclear or incorrectly represents the problem.
Does the student solve the problem correctly?	Yes, the student generates more than one correct solution.	Yes, the student gives one correct solution.	No, the student gives no correct solution.

Looking for Evidence of Understanding

Jasmine: Low Level

Jasmine started by drawing a row of people across the top of her page. Once she ran out of room, she counted them, "Eight." She started a new row, and drew three more people before counting again from 1 to 11. "I need one more." The teacher did not understand Jasmine's drawing and asked her to record her solution. Jasmine wrote, "12 kids. 2 rows." Jasmine did not show a clear understanding of the problem and incorrectly represented the situation by solving it with two rows that are unequal in length.

Valerie: Moderate Level

Valerie drew two rows of five chairs each and then said, "I need to count. I need twelve." After realizing that she had drawn only ten chairs, she said, "I need two more to make twelve." She started to draw a third row, and the teacher said, "What do you know about the rows?" Valerie said, "Oops, I have to have the same number in each, and that one would only have two. I guess I can put one more in each row." As she added the last two chairs, she said, "Of course! Six and six is twelve." The teacher then asked, "Is there another answer?" Valerie answered confidently, "No, that's all. Six and six is twelve."

Ladonna: High Level

Ladonna's drawing and writing clearly showed her understanding of the problem and of equal groupings. She gave two different but related solutions: "4 rows, 3 in each row" and "3 rows, 4 in each row."

Variations for the Range of Learners

- Present the problem with a smaller or larger number of people.
- Revise the problem so that it has only one correct solution, by specifying either a given number of rows or a given number of people in each row.

2

Algebra

YOUNG children delight in clapping their hands or stomping their feet in rhythmic patterns. They enjoy repetitive songs, rhythmic chants, and predictive poems that are based on repeating and growing patterns. They tend to make patterns with blocks during playtime, alternating blocks of different sizes or different colors as they build pattern trains. They naturally engage in sorting objects by size and number, oftentimes even sorting objects by specific attributes. They revel in explaining the pattern they built or saw and how they might extend a given pattern. The patterns and patterning activities in which young children readily engage serve to form the basis of their emergent algebraic reasoning. The development of algebraic concepts evolves and continues to develop as children move from prekindergarten through second grade.

Arithmetic and algebra are both useful for describing important relationships in the world. "But although arithmetic is effective in describing static pictures of the world, algebra is dynamic and a necessary vehicle for describing a changing world. Even young children can appreciate the significance of change and the need to describe variation" (Greenes, Cavanagh, Dacey, Findell, and Small, 2001, p. 1). In that spirit, using patterns as the focal point of algebraic thinking in the prekindergarten–grade 2 classroom highlights for students possible changes, predictable situations, and opportunities to generalize about their own developing understanding in mathematics. Whether children are snapping color cubes together in a predictable way or observing the relationship between numbers and operations through activities with input-output machines, young children are eager to experience, and are capable of identifying and describing, change. As young students generalize from observations about number and operations, they are forming the basis of their algebraic thinking.

The assessment tasks in this chapter have been designed and selected for their alignment with the NCTM Algebra Standards and Expectations for prekindergarten–grade 2 (NCTM, 2000). Our hope is that those tasks open a window to young students' knowledge of algebraic reasoning and foster teachers' insights into the thinking and reasoning of their students. As with any assessment, teachers need to think about why they select a particular task, how they might wish to adjust the task for their students, and how they are going to use the information to monitor and further support the development of students' mathematical knowledge.

Algebra Assessment Items

Standard: Understand patterns, relations, and functions

Expectation: Recognize, describe, and extend patterns, such as sequences of sounds and shapes or simple numeric patterns, and translate from one representation to another

1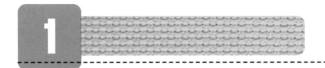

What Comes Next?

Grade range: Prekindergarten–kindergarten

About the mathematics: Young children tend to be extremely inquisitive. They spend time observing, mimicking, and copying that which they see around them. As a result, they have acquired reasoning and discriminatory skills that are important components in developing algebraic thinking—copying patterns, extending patterns, and creating patterns of their own. The "What Comes Next?" task engages students in extending a pattern of colored cubes. They are asked to build on the pattern they observe in the row of cubes. The essential part of this task is for the student to identify one or more cubes that would make sense when added to those they see—that is, to extend the pattern started by the teacher.

TASK

I have snapped together some cubes (e.g., a row of green, blue, green, blue, green, blue).

Look carefully. Can you add on a cube that goes with what you see?

Can you add another cube? Another? More?

Why did you pick those cubes?

Using this assessment task: This task is designed for use with individual students, allowing the teacher to see immediately which cubes the student selects. The teacher thus has an opportunity to ask probing questions to determine how the child is reasoning about his or her choices. The teacher will need to provide a preestablished pattern made from connecting cubes and to supply additional cubes for the student. Snap together a row of cubes with at least three repetitions of a repeating pattern having an ABAB structure. The container of cubes from which the students are to select the next cube needs to contain cubes of the same colors as those used in the pattern but should also include cubes of several other colors.

Avoid calling the row of cubes a *pattern* unless students have familiarity with this specific terminology. Very young children may be able to recognize and offer an idea about what might come next in a pattern without knowing the vocabulary associated with patterning. They can look at a sequence of colors or shapes and predict what might be the next piece in the sequence. A helpful tactic for the teachers is to record notes from their observation on the assessment record supplied on the blackline master "What Comes Next? Observation Form." Teachers may also need to have a few different "patterns" ready to offer a child more than one opportunity to show his or her thinking. Some teachers change the colors used in the pattern in the event a child has seen the work of a previous student. They are mindful to always use the same ABAB structure so the assessment task is equitable for every child.

Solution: The solutions will vary from student to student. A complete solution includes evidence that a student can successfully add on at least three cubes to the ABAB pattern the teacher started and can offer some reasoning for how that choice was derived.

Continuum of Understanding

No Evidence

Gives no response or an incorrect response; for example, may break apart the set of cubes offered by the teacher and reply, "I like to build like this," then begin to snap together random cubes with no apparent evidence of the idea of patterning

Limited Evidence

Adds on one cube and says that he or she does not want to do any more, or adds on one repetition of the core unit of the pattern but indicates that no more additions are possible

Adequate Evidence

Adds on three cubes that correctly follow the pattern the teacher started; also describes some way of knowing that he or she is following a rule based on color, for example, may say, "After green comes blue."

Strong Evidence

Adds on at least three cubes that correctly follow the pattern the teacher started, and demonstrates that the pattern can continue on and on; is able to describe how she or he added on cubes on the basis of repetition of the colors, and indicates the infinite possibility of the task, for example, may say, "It has to be green then blue then green then blue. It goes on forever."

Looking for Evidence of Understanding

After assessing his prekindergarten pupils, one teacher stated, "I felt comfortable determining a level of understanding, since I watched and listened to every one of my students and kept a record of the conversation." He noted that some children easily added on to the pattern he had made and were eager to keep adding more cubes. For other children, the task was very difficult. He commented, "I could see in their demeanor that I was asking too much of them. Even though some of these kids could show me what comes next, they didn't have the language or reasoning skills to say much about how this works."

Curtis: No Evidence

	Yes	No	Comments
Adds next piece in pattern		✓	"I like red!"
Is able to continue the pattern with additional pieces		✓	C. adds 3 more red cubes and is all done.
Demonstrates an understanding of how the pattern works		✓	
Articulates why specified pieces were added to the pattern		✓	Work with C. on some activities for
Describes the repeating core of the pattern		✓	copying pattern.

Curtis remarked that he liked red and then snapped on three red cubes. He did not show any awareness of the green-blue pattern presented by the teacher.

Benjamin: Limited Evidence

	Yes	No	Comments
Adds next piece in pattern	✓		Snaps on green
Is able to continue the pattern with additional pieces	✓ ?		Snaps on blue and stops,
Demonstrates an understanding of how the pattern works	✓		"All done!"
Articulates why specified pieces were added to the pattern	?		B. was very fidgety and stopped after 2 cubes — assess at another time
Describes the repeating core of the pattern	?		

Benjamin added a green cube. After being prompted, he then added a blue cube. When prompted again, he announced, "All done."

Jade: Strong Evidence

	Yes	No	Comments
Adds next piece in pattern	✓		
Is able to continue the pattern with additional pieces	✓		
Demonstrates an understanding of how the pattern works	✓		"It goes green, then blue, green then blue."
Articulates why specified pieces were added to the pattern	✓		"I can't use red... no reds!"
Describes the repeating core of the pattern	✓		"It's only green and blue over and over... forever."

Jade readily and correctly extended the pattern. She knew the pattern was composed of only green and blue cubes and that it could be continued forever.

Variations for the Range of Learners

- If the child does not seem to understand the directions, model for him or her how you created the pattern. Without describing your thoughts, ask the child to carefully watch what you do with the cubes. Add on one or two more cubes, and then determine whether the student is ready to give the task a try.

- Vary the structure of the repeating pattern, for example, use AB, ABC, ABB, or AAB patterns.
- Some students may have difficulty snapping cubes together. In such a situation, vary the material so that students line up colored cubes or shapes on a surface.
- Some students may not be able to discriminate by color. In that event, vary the material by using different types of common objects or shapes (e.g., an object pattern of button, key, button, key or a shape pattern of triangle, square, circle; triangle, square, circle).
- Show more repetitions in the pattern you create.

Standard: Understand patterns, relations, and functions

Expectation: Recognize, describe, and extend patterns, such as sequences of sounds and shapes or simple numeric patterns, and translate from one representation to another

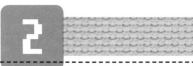

Making Patterns: Same or Different?

Grade range: K–2

About the mathematics: Copying, extending, and creating patterns form an integral part of the mathematics curriculum for young children. Patterns are a way for young students to recognize order and to organize their world. Students develop the ability to form generalizations about patterns by the type of questions that teachers ask. In this task students are asked to generate two different patterns and to explain how they are the same or different. When comparing the structures of their patterns, students need to consider how each representation can be generalized. Rather than think that two patterns are the same because they both use red and blue, students can translate or generalize about how two patterns are the same or different on the basis of their structure, that is, the way in which they repeat or grow.

TASK

Use a manipulative of your choice (e.g., connecting cubes, animal counters) to create two different patterns.

What is the same about how your patterns work? What is different?

Using this assessment task: This task is designed for use with individual students. Each student will need physical materials, such as connecting cubes, teddy bear counters, or pattern blocks, to create her or his patterns. The materials should be of various colors because young children often use color as the discriminating attribute in their patterns. Use the blackline master "Making Patterns Observation Form" for recording student work and reasoning. If students are capable of generating patterns on paper, the teacher may want to provide a recording sheet for their work. In addition, the teacher can ask students to write about how their patterns are the same or different.

An important skill to assess is whether students are able to generate any type of pattern, whether very simple or more complex. Also important to ascertain is whether students have some way of determining how the two patterns they create are the same or different. If students begin to explain that their patterns are different because they used different colors, be sure to ask questions that elicit an understanding about the core unit of the pattern, for example, "What else do you notice about your pattern?" Sometimes one attribute (e.g., color, shape) may be so compelling that students need a little nudge to move them beyond focusing on that aspect so that they can describe the core unit of repetition in their pattern.

Solution: Solutions will vary from student to student. A complete solution includes evidence that a student can construct two patterns with different structures and then describe how the two patterns are different in structure. Students in kindergarten through second grade usually construct repeating patterns that are based on core units of AB, ABC, AAB, or ABB. Some students may generate a growing pattern, for example, ABBCCCDDDD.

Continuum of Understanding

No Understanding

Gives no response or an incorrect response, for example, may snap a random set of color cubes together and identify the result as a pattern without reflecting the idea that a pattern repeats or grows in some predictable way

Limited Understanding

Generates one pattern, and indicates that it is the only pattern he or she knows how to make or the only pattern that is possible; may believe that a pattern has an ABAB structure and thus that any other arrangement is not a pattern

Strong Understanding

Generates two patterns with different structures, for example, an ABAB and an ABC pattern; can explain how the structures are different by comparing the core repeating elements

Advanced Understanding

Is able to generalize about how patterns repeat and grow by indicating that many arrangements are possible; identifies the core repeating element or the manner in which her or his pattern grows, and explains how it can be modified to be the same as, or different from, the pattern with which it is being compared

Looking for Evidence of Understanding

After assessing her first graders, one teacher noted, "We had just completed a series of lessons targeting the ideas of pattern, and this assessment met my needs in determining how and at what level of understanding my students were thinking about patterns." The students used connecting cubes to build their patterns. The teacher used the observation form to record her students' patterns and to make notes on their responses to her question "How are your patterns the same of different?"

Student	2 patterns student generates	# times each core repeats	Pattern is predictable?	What is the same?	What is different?
Alexis	G B R / G G B B R R	3 / 2	yes / yes	"They both use 3 colors."	"One goes green blue, red the other has 2 of each color."
Tyrek	Bl Y	7 / —	yes / —	"I made a bumble bee. It's really long."	no response ⓣ Can you make another – "NO!"
Raymond	O Y R B / O Y Y	3 / 4	yes / yes	"They both start with orange and yellow."	"One keeps going with 2 more colors and then repeats. This is OYY over over."
Ann	G Bl / R B	5 / 5	yes / yes	"They are both 10 and use 2 colors."	"They use different colors."

Tyrek and Ann: Underdeveloped Understanding

Tyrek used a core unit of black-yellow to make one AB pattern, which he called his "bumblebee pattern." He did not produce a second pattern even when prompted. Ann made two AB patterns. Her first pattern had a core unit of green-black, and her second pattern had a core unit of red-blue. She reasoned that her patterns were different because they used different colors.

Alexis and Raymond: Complete Understanding

Alexis made an "ABC" pattern using green-blue-red. Then she made an "AABBCC" pattern using green-green-blue-blue-red-red. She used the same colors in each pattern but could identify how the structure in each differed. Raymond readily made two patterns with different structures. His ABCD pattern used orange-yellow-red-blue, and his ABB pattern used orange-yellow-yellow. He could distinguish between the patterns and noted that both would keep going, or continue over and over.

Variations for the Range of Learners

- Ask students to generate only one pattern and to describe how it works.
- Present a pattern, and ask students to generate one that is different. Have them explain how they know that their patterns are different.
- Directly ask students to make a pattern with a specific unit to be repeated, and then ask them to create a second pattern that is the same as, or different from, their first one.
- Create two different patterns of your own, and ask students to explain how they are the same or different. Some teachers prefer to give a task such as this one, which is somewhat less open-ended than the others, so that they can observe the range of student responses to the more closely defined task.

Standard: Understand patterns, relations, and functions

Expectation: Analyze how repeating patterns are generated

3

Fixing Patterns

Grade range: K–2

About the mathematics: The "Fixing Patterns" task fosters insight into students' understanding of patterns and relationships by asking them to consider, on the basis of limited information, possibilities for how a pattern might have been constructed. Students are given a three-color sequence. They may reason that that sequence is the core unit, and repeat it three more times to fulfill the criterion of using twelve cubes. Other students may generate a pattern with additional colors. The task highlights fundamental aspects of algebraic thinking, in that it requires students to generalize or reason indirectly as they consider the information to determine a final solution.

TASK

I made a pattern by snapping together 12 connecting cubes. Then it fell apart. All I have left of my pattern are 3 of the cubes I snapped together. They look like this.

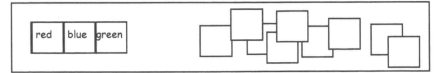

Draw a picture of what my pattern might have looked like.

Might it have looked any other way? Describe your thinking, and show another possibility if one exists.

Using this assessment task: This task can be used with individuals, with small groups of students, or with the whole class. Make a copy of the "Fixing Patterns" blackline master for each student. Some teachers choose to have connecting cubes available for students. The assortment should include red, blue, and green cubes, as well as cubes of several other colors. If students are not able to read the color words on the blackline master, a teacher could color in the first three squares or direct children to do so as they begin the task. Demonstrate that three of the cubes from the pattern are still connected, and hold up an example of a red-blue-green cube sequence. Some teachers have found that some sort of dramatization of the broken-pattern scenario is helpful in engaging students with this task. Those teachers have noted that many students are familiar with the frustration that occurs when something they have worked hard to make falls apart. This assessment task capitalizes on the experience of having a pattern fall apart and the necessity of recreating the pattern on the basis of limited information.

Solution: Several solutions to this problem are possible, including the following examples:

- Use a three-cube core unit of red-blue-green, and repeat it four times.
- Use a four-cube core unit, and repeat it three times. In this variation, students are able to consider that other colors may have been used, such as red-blue-green-black or pink-red-blue-green.
- Use a six-cube core unit, and repeat it twice (e.g., red-blue-green-yellow-yellow-black).

A student may raise the possibility of a solution in which the final repetition is not completed. Teachers will need to consider the rationale of the student if he or she offers such a solution, for example, a five-cube core unit of red-blue-green-black-brown. For that sequence, two complete repetitions can be displayed, but only part of the third repetition, because of the limitation of using exactly twelve cubes. The teacher's openness to a variety of possible solutions is important to the success of the task, so the main emphasis should be placed on how students are thinking and how they defend their choices.

Continuum of Understanding

No Understanding

- Gives no response; may not believe that the task is doable, or may think that she or he does not have sufficient understanding of the concept of patterning to make a reasonable attempt
- Produces an incorrect response; may consider the red-blue-green sequence as being composed of random colors and so may snap on more cubes of those and other colors in a random fashion; may or may not consider the criterion of using twelve cubes

Underdeveloped Understanding

- Creates a pattern with twelve cubes, but does not consider the criterion of the known color sequence
- Snaps together cubes on the basis of the known color sequence (i.e., red-blue-green cubes) but does not repeat the sequence to make a pattern
- Is able to create one pattern, usually a three-cube core unit of red-blue-green, but cannot create a second pattern based on the given criteria

Complete Understanding

- Is able to generate two patterns that meet all the criteria
- Can explain why the solutions work

Advanced Understanding

- Clearly demonstrates an understanding of the complexity of this task, can illustrate multiple ways to solve this problem, and can explain how and why the arrangements represent solutions; goes beyond the recognition of how two patterns can be made, and is beginning to generalize the ideas embedded in constructing and interpreting patterns

Looking for Evidence of Understanding

In using this task, most students seemed clear about the criterion of using exactly twelve cubes. However, some students did not realize they could use additional colors or that they could use a core unit that was larger than the three-unit sequence composed of only the red, blue, and green cubes snapped together.

Amy: Underdeveloped Understanding

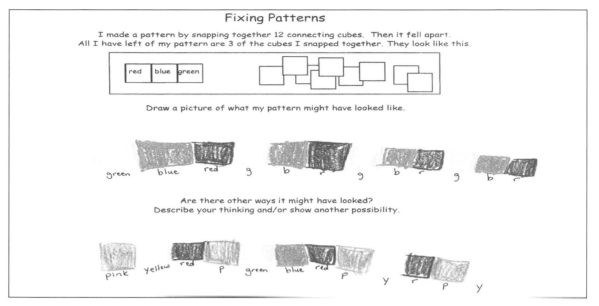

Amy's work indicated that she has some ideas of how repeating patterns work, but when asked for a second way, she seemed to be less secure in her ideas. Amy completed one pattern but reversed the order of the colors. She then generated a new arrangement using twelve cubes. When asked to describe her arrangement, Amy replied, "I need twelve cubes. I have green, blue, red, but I like pink, yellow, and red."

David: Underdeveloped Understanding

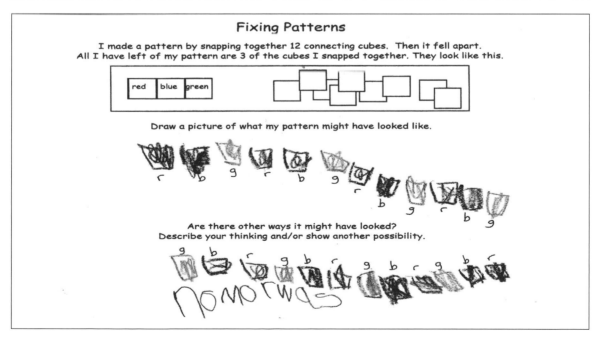

David responded to this task as did most of the children in the class. He was clear about the criterion of using twelve cubes, and kept the red, blue, and green cubes snapped together. For his second pattern, he merely flipped the pattern order so that the core unit became green-blue-red. In one way, his interpretation could be considered correct if he had explained that the pattern order might have flipped when it broke apart. However, his understanding remained underdeveloped, as evidenced by his claim of "No more ways."

Bethany: Complete Understanding

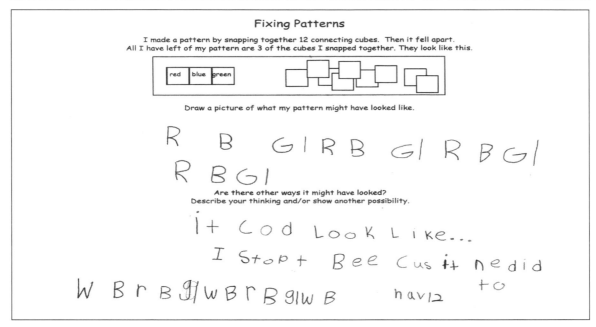

Bethany met all the criteria of the task, showed a complete understanding of pattern, and used words to explain her thinking. The teacher was impressed that Bethany used a line to separate the repeating units in both of her patterns. She showed four repetitions of red-blue-green for the first pattern. For her second pattern, she used a five-cube core unit of white-blue-red-blue-green, and showed two complete repetitions and part of a third repetition. For her explanation she wrote, "I stopped because it needed to have 12."

Charlie: Advanced Understanding

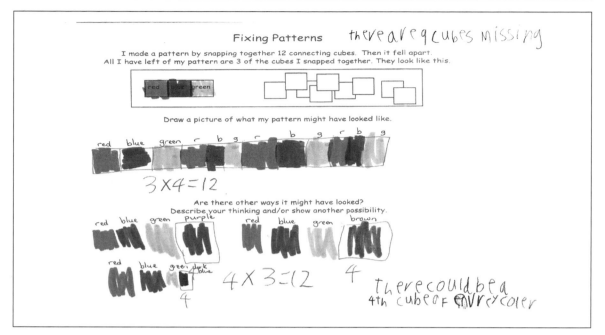

Charlie connected multiplication with his ideas of how patterns repeat. He was reasoning about how many repetitions of a given number of cubes were needed to have a total of twelve cubes. For his first pattern, he repeated a three-cube unit (red-blue-green) four times and wrote $3 \times 4 = 12$. In the second pattern, he reversed this expression and repeated a four-cube unit three times, writing $4 \times 3 = 12$. Charlie was also beginning to generalize his observations when he wrote, "There could be a 4th cube of every color." He was moving beyond needing the specific colors as a context and had begun to see how structures of patterns are similar.

Variations for the Range of Learners

This task can be simplified by presenting a two-color sequence (e.g., yellow-blue) and leaving two repetitions intact, or by limiting the number of possible repetitions of the pattern. In a similar way, this task can be made more challenging by increasing the number of colors in the sequence.

Standard: Understand patterns, relations, and functions

Expectations
- Analyze how repeating patterns are generated
- Use the language of mathematics to express mathematical ideas precisely

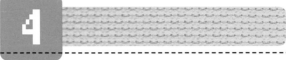

Growing Creature

Grade range: Grades 1–2

About the mathematics: In the "Growing Creature" task, students are asked to create a growing pattern and communicate how the pattern grows by using words, numbers, or diagrams. A growing pattern is structurally different from a repeating pattern. Each element in the pattern grows or increases in a predictable way. For example a growing pattern follows a rule that determines the change that needs to take place. The numeric pattern of 1, 4, 7, 10, 13 follows the rule of adding 3 to an element or number to determine the next element. For example, adding 1 + 3 results in 4, adding 4 + 3 results in 7, adding 7 + 3 results in 10, and so on. Young students may not have had as much experience with growing patterns as they have had with repeating patterns, but they are usually able to draw pictures or use counting or computation to determine the next element in a given growing pattern. Experience with both types of patterns helps students develop algebraic reasoning and generalization skills.

TASK

1. On day 1, 5 squares are needed to build the creature. It grows the same amount each day. What will it look like on day 2 and on day 3?

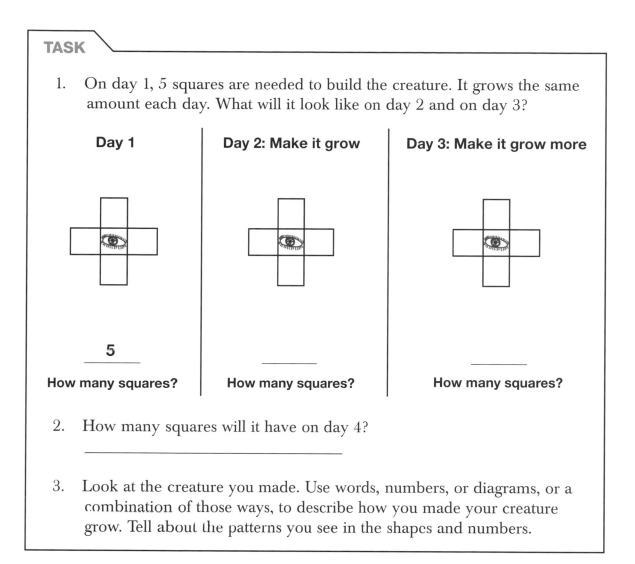

| **Day 1** | **Day 2: Make it grow** | **Day 3: Make it grow more** |

5

How many squares? | **How many squares?** | **How many squares?**

2. How many squares will it have on day 4?

3. Look at the creature you made. Use words, numbers, or diagrams, or a combination of those ways, to describe how you made your creature grow. Tell about the patterns you see in the shapes and numbers.

Source: Adapted from *Navigating through Algebra in Prekindergarten–Grade 2,* by Carole Greenes, Mary Cavanagh, Linda Dacey, Carol Findell, and Marian Small (Reston, Va.: National Council of Teachers of Mathematics, 2001).

Using this assessment task: This task can be used with a whole class. Each student will need a copy of the "Growing Creature" blackline master. Students should complete the task individually. Provide students with physical materials, such as square tiles or paper squares, to create concrete models of their growing creatures.

Solution

Question 1: Several growing patterns are possible. A successful pattern increases by the same quantity each successive day (i.e., the same number of blocks are added each time). Some possible solutions are shown. The orange squares show what was added on day 2, and the gray squares show what was added on day 3. Example A adds four squares each day. Example B also adds four squares each day but in a different configuration. Example C grows by two squares, and example D grows by one square each day. Example E grows in a completely different way, by replicating the original configuration of five squares.

Examples of Possible Solutions

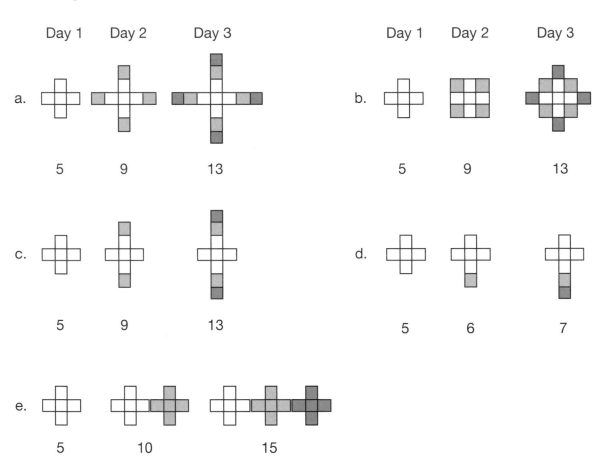

Question 2. The number of squares needed on day 4 will depend on the pattern generated. The increase in the number of squares required will be consistent with the previous steps taken to make the creature grow.

Question 3. Look for descriptions of the number of squares added each day and how the shape of the pattern grows.

Continuum of Understanding

Insufficient Understanding

Seems to add a random number of squares to show the growth of the creature; does not refer to the pattern numerically nor describe how it grows, for example, "My creature has a tail that keeps growing and growing. I like my creature."

Partially Proficient Understanding

Shows a creature that grows in a consistent manner each day but may not be able to describe the specific pattern; may indicate the rate of growth each day but may make an error in calculating the total number of squares

Proficient Understanding

Shows the pattern of how the creature grows in a consistent manner, and is able to describe its growth in both shape and quantity

Looking for Evidence of Understanding

Stephen: Insufficient Understanding

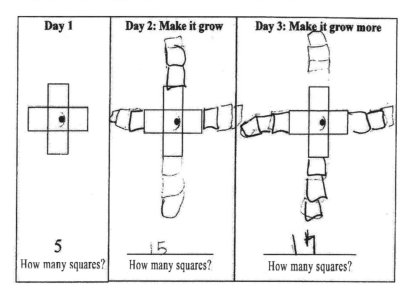

Stephen made an attempt to have the creature grow. However, the numbers he wrote to show the changes in the number of squares are not accurate. No other work appears on the paper.

Grace: Partially Proficient Understanding

Grace showed and described a creature that grows by four squares each time, but she made an error in determining the number of squares needed for day 4.

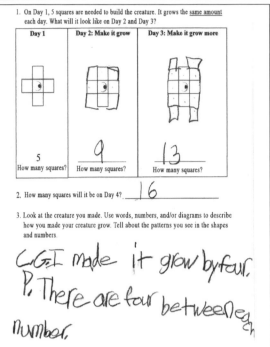

Samantha and Mitchell: Proficient Understanding

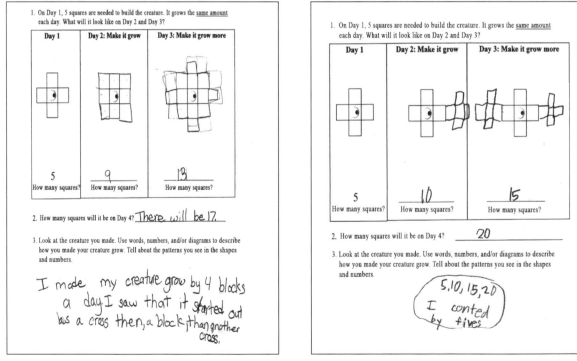

Samantha

Mitchell

Samantha and Mitchell both demonstrated an understanding of how their unique creature grows in a consistent pattern. Samantha described how her creature changes both in shape and in quantity. Mitchell replicated the original configuration and added five more squares each time, alternating the side to which they were added.

Variations for the Range of Learners

The growing-creature assessment task assumes that students have had experiences with examining and building growing patterns. To simply the task for students with limited experiences, provide a starting figure that grows more predictably and in only one direction, along with the figures for day 2 and day 3. Ask students to show the creature in days 4 and 5 and to describe how it grew. Possible starters are as follows:

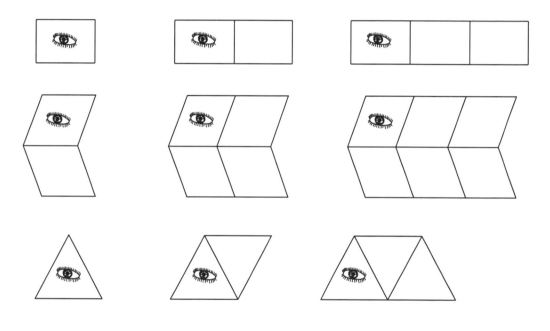

Standard: Analyze change in various contexts

Expectation: Describe quantitative change

5

How Much Is It Worth?

Grade range: 1–2

About the mathematics: Seeing how one element relates to another is one way of thinking algebraically. In the "How Much Is It Worth?" task students are asked to consider how a given value of the triangle in a set of pattern blocks relates to the value of the hexagon. Students alter the value of the triangle, then consider what effect that change has on the value of the hexagon. Money is used to accentuate the value, or worth, of the blocks in this task.

TASK

Use triangles and hexagons from a set of pattern blocks to solve this problem. Use pictures, numbers, or words, or a combination of those ways, to explain your thinking.

1. If 1 triangle is worth 2¢, how much is 1 hexagon worth?
2. What happens if the triangle is worth 5¢? How much is 1 hexagon worth?
3. How much are 2 hexagons worth?

Using this assessment task: This task is designed to be used with a whole class or in small groups. Each student will need a copy of the "How Much Is It Worth?" blackline master and some triangles and hexagons from a set of pattern blocks. Teachers may also want to provide paper cutouts for students to glue down as a way to help record their reasoning. Students will need to have had some previous experience with pattern blocks or be given time to explore with them before being asked to focus on this task. By determining the six-to-one relationship of triangles to hexagons, students can then assign a value to the triangles as a way of determining the value of the hexagon.

Solution

Question 1: If 1 triangle is worth 2 cents, 1 hexagon is worth 12 cents.

Question 2: If 1 triangle is worth 5 cents, 1 hexagon is worth 30 cents.

Question 3: If 2 triangles are worth 5 cents, 2 hexagons are worth 60 cents. Students' explanations will vary but should demonstrate an understanding of the six-to-one relationship of the triangles to the hexagon. Students may reason using counting by ones, skip counting, repeated addition, known addition facts, or known multiplication facts.

Continuum of Understanding

Little or No Understanding

- Makes no response, or attempts to construct an arrangement with pattern blocks but shows no awareness of the problem or how to solve it

Underdeveloped Understanding

- Realizes that several triangles can be used to equal a hexagon and may even determine that number to be 6 but is then not sure how to proceed with the task
- Gives an incorrect value because of a calculation error
- Completes the first part of this task on the basis of 2 cents, but cannot make the leap to the second part of the task when the value of the triangle changes to 5 cents

Complete Understanding

- Provides an accurate solution to all parts of the task; demonstrates an understanding of the changing relationships when the value changes from 2 cents to 5 cents and when the number of hexagons changes from 1 to 2

Advanced Understanding

- Demonstrates proficiency in all aspects of this task; also recognizes and describes the patterns and relationships that emerge and can extend them to additional hexagons and other values of the triangle

Looking for Evidence of Understanding

After reviewing student work from a combined first–second-grade class, the teacher commented, "I was very pleased with the overall performance of my students on this assessment. I did have a few students who could not make sense of the problem. I don't know if it was the money that confused them or if they really do not have a handle yet on relationships. I will make a note for trying this assessment with them again at the end of the year after we have had more experience learning about money and patterns and using the pattern blocks." The teacher noted that many students were able to give a correct numerical response, but they ranged greatly in how well they were able to record their thinking and explain the relationships.

Abraham: Little or No Understanding

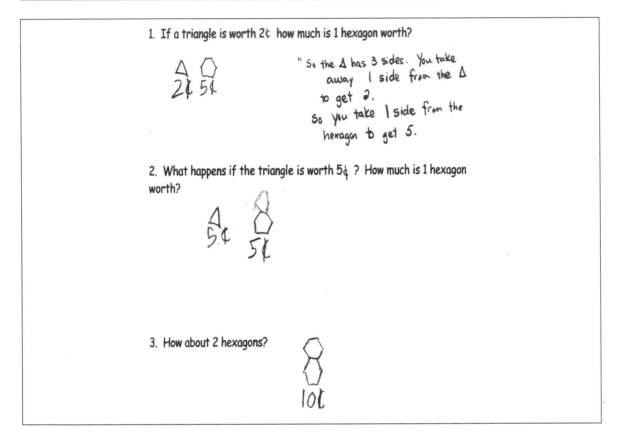

Abraham attempted to make sense of the situation by using some knowledge of triangles and hexagons. Abraham verbalized, "So the triangle has three sides. You take away one side from the triangle to get two. So you take away one side from the hexagon to get five." The teacher wrote Abraham's response on his paper as a record of his thinking. In the second question, he stated that the hexagon was still worth five cents. On the basis of that value, Abraham was aware of the idea of doubling the value of one hexagon to get the value of two hexagons.

Karen: Underdeveloped or Complete Understanding

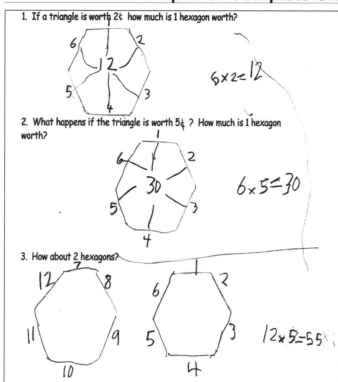

Karen's representation clearly demonstrated complete understanding of the situation, but because of a calculation error in the third question, she did not get the correct answer. Teachers will need to judge a response of this kind on the basis of their knowledge of the student's capabilities. Some teachers may conclude that the student has underdeveloped understanding because of the calculation error. Other teachers may conclude complete understanding because all other aspects of the work indicate a solid level of understanding of the relationships in the situation.

Zoe: Complete Understanding

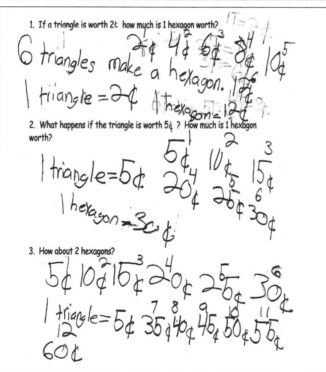

Zoe demonstrated awareness of the relationships in the situation and stayed focused on the ratios. By writing "6 triangles make a hexagon," Zoe showed the constant relationship of the triangle to the hexagon. By noting "1 triangle = 2¢" and then later "1 triangle = 5¢," she demonstrated an awareness of the changing monetary relationships in the task. Zoe used a systematic way of keeping track of each relationship; her approach seems to be a foundation for moving toward advanced understanding.

Variations for the Range of Learners

- Break the task into more steps. For example, "If a triangle is worth 1 cent, how much is the hexagon worth?" or "If a triangle is worth 2 cents, what are two triangles worth?"
- Use other blocks from the set of pattern blocks (e.g., use the relationship of the trapezoid to the hexagon), or change the monetary value of the triangle or other initial block.

Standard: Represent and analyze mathematical situations and structures using algebraic symbols

Expectation: Demonstrate an understanding of conventional symbolic notation, specifically the equals sign, and the use of variables as unknowns

What Goes in the □?

Grade range: 1–2

About the mathematics: The "What Goes in the □?" task lends insight into students' understanding of the equals sign as a symbol of equivalence or balance. Young students typically perceive the equals sign as a signal to perform some action on the numbers and often explain that it tells you "where to put the answer." Students should realize that the equals sign indicates a relationship in which the quantities on each side balance, or have the same value.

TASK

What number would you put in the □ to make the following a true number sentence?

$$8 + 4 = □ + 5$$

How did you figure out your answer?

Source: Adapted from *Thinking Mathematically: Integrating Arithmetic and Algebra in Elementary School,* by Thomas P., Carpenter, Megan L. Franke, and Linda Levi (Portsmouth, NH: Heinemann, 2003).

Using this assessment task: The task can be presented to individual students, small groups, or the whole class. Each student will need a copy of the "What Goes in the □?" blackline master. Younger students may need to be prompted to further explain their reasoning or their confusion, for example, "Tell me what you are thinking about or wondering about." The teacher can then record the response on the student's paper.

Solution: The solution, or the number that goes in the box, is 7. Students' responses for how they figured out the answer will vary but should provide evidence that they realize that the equation needs to balance, so the amount expressed on the left side of the equals sign needs to have the same value as, or be equivalent to, the amount expressed on the right side of the equals sign.

Continuum of Understanding

Limited Understanding

- Gives no response or an incorrect response
- Gives an answer of 12, completely ignoring the "+ 5"; explains that that you have to add 8 + 4 and then put the answer after the equals sign

Underdeveloped Understanding

- Indicates that he or she does not know how to solve this type of problem
- Shows confusion by the "+ 5" on the right side of the equals sign
- Gives an answer of 17, and explains that you have to add all the numbers

Complete Understanding

- Gives the correct response of 7
- Explains that the equals sign represents a balance between the quantities on each side
- Compares the two sides of the equals sign by completing the computations, for example, adds 8 + 4 = 12 and then reasons to find a number that when added to 5 equals 12

Advanced Understanding

- Is able to compare the mathematical expressions without actually carrying out the computations, for example, reasons that since 5 is one more than 4, the missing number must be one less than 8

Looking for Evidence of Understanding

After reviewing the work of her students on this task, one teacher was surprised that about three-fourths of her class performed at either the limited or the under-developed level. She commented, "I appreciate their perseverance to make sense of it in some way, but this assessment certainly tells me that I need to do some thinking about how I am helping children make sense of the equal[s] sign. Of the 25% who did give the correct response, I felt only two students were at an advanced understanding level."

Wilfred and Donna: Underdeveloped Understanding

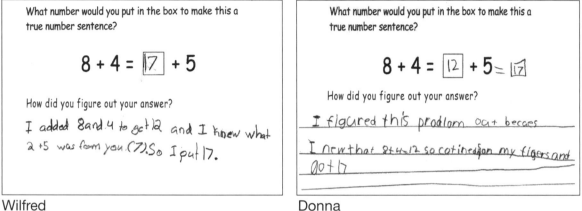

Wilfred

Donna

Wilfred and Donna both saw the task as a string of three numbers to be added. Wilfred's work shows that at first he printed 12 in the box, but he seemed to correct his error by adding on 5 more. The 17 is then shown over the erased 12. Donna simply added an additional equals sign and box to make sense of the problem. Many students in the class expressed confusion, as one student explained, "I can't figure it out with this [points to the + 5] because I usually just do three numbers."

Carly: Complete Understanding

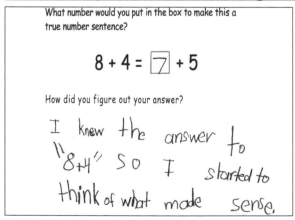

Carly indicated that "making sense" was the driving force to the solution for her. When prompted she explained further, "The equal[s] sign means both things are the same, and $8 + 4 = 12$ and $7 + 5 = 12$."

Terry: Advanced Understanding

What number would you put in the box to make this a true number sentence?

$$8 + 4 = \boxed{7} + 5$$

How did you figure out your answer?

5 is more then 4
8 is more Then 7

Terry recorded 7 correctly as the missing number and tried to describe the relationship she was noticing—that 5 was "one" more than 5, so 8 must be "one" more than the missing number, which makes it 7.

Variations for the Range of Learners

- Use smaller or larger numbers in the equation, for example, $2 + 3 = \square + 4$ or $25 + 33 = \square + 26$.
- Use other operations or multiple operations.
- Place the unknown in different positions.

Standard: Represent and analyze mathematical situations and structures using algebraic symbols

Expectations:
- Illustrate general principles and properties of operations, such as commutativity, using specific numbers
- Use concrete, pictorial, and verbal representations to develop an understanding of invented and conventional symbolic notations

True and False Number Sentences

Grade range: 1–2

About the mathematics: This task challenges students' existing conceptions about the meaning and use of the equals sign. Students often believe that number sentences must be of the form $a + b = c$, with a single number to the right of the equals sign. In this task students are presented with a variety of true number sentences that are not in the familiar form and that include one false number sentence. In each of the number sentences, students need to realize that the equals sign indicates a relationship in which the amount on the left side is the "same as" the amount on the right side of the equals sign.

TASK

For each number sentence, tell whether it is true or false. How do you know?

a.	$5 + 4 = 9$	True	False
b.	$9 = 5 + 4$	True	False
c.	$9 = 9$	True	False
d.	$5 + 4 = 4 + 5$	True	False
e.	$5 + 4 = 5 + 4$	True	False
f.	$5 + 4 = 6 + 3$	True	False
g.	$5 + 5 = 5 + 6$	True	False

Source: Adapted from *Thinking Mathematically: Integrating Arithmetic and Algebra in Elementary School,* by Thomas P. Carpenter, Megan L. Franke, and Linda Levi (Portsmouth, NH: Heinemann, 2003).

Using this assessment task: Each student will need a copy of the "True-False Number Sentences" blackline master. If students do not have experience with classifying number sentences as true or false, introduce the idea with simple computations (e.g., 2 + 1 = 3, 4 + 4 = 7) and discuss what we mean when we say that a number sentence is true or false. Teachers may choose to present the number sentences together as a complete set or to present one number sentence at a time to students individually, in small groups, or in a whole-class gathering. Students may need to be prompted to further explain their reasoning in follow-up discussions. Some teachers find that making notes on the student sheet as a student dictates his or her reasoning is a helpful tactic.

Solution

a. 5 + 4 = 9   (True)
b. 9 = 5 + 4   (True)
c. 9 = 9   (True)
d. 5 + 4 = 4 + 5   (True)
e. 5 + 4 = 5 + 4   (True)
f. 5 + 4 = 6 + 3   (True)
g. 5 + 5 = 5 + 6   (False)

Students' explanations will vary but should include evidence that the student is reasoning about the equals sign as a balance indicating that the amount on the left side is the "same as" the amount on the right side.

Continuum of Understanding

Not Yet Started or Ready

*   Gives no response, or responds that most of the number sentences are false

Beginning Understanding

*   Identifies some of the number sentences as true and some as false
*   Accepts as true some number sentences that are not of the form $a + b = c$
*   Agrees that the numbers represented by the expressions on either side of the equals sign are the same, but may still believe that the variations are not true number sentences

On Target

*   Correctly identifies the number sentences as true or false
*   Explains that the equals sign indicates that the two sides balance or that the expressions on both sides represent the same quantity
*   Compares the two sides of the equals sign by completing the computations, for example, explains that 5 + 4 and 4 + 5 both equal 9

Going Beyond

- Compares the mathematical expressions without actually carrying out the computations, and reasons using properties of the operations; for example, reasons that adding $5 + 4$ gives the same answer as $4 + 5$ and does not need to find their sum

Looking for Evidence of Understanding

After giving this task to her students, a teacher commented, "The way my students talked about these problems was fascinating. They were very puzzled and bothered by the way the problems were written." The teacher walked around as the students were working to see what was happening and to listen to what they might be saying. She noticed that a few students circled true for the first number sentence and then rather quickly circled false for all the rest. The students seemed to barely look at the problems. She asked one child about this who replied, "They just don't look right, so they have to be false." Another child said, "They seem backwards."

Another teacher added, "This assessment task was a good check in to see how children are really making sense of our standard notations and symbols. It makes me see that I need to develop more lessons that focus on these ideas."

Xander: Not Yet Started

Xander circled true for the first and third problems and false for all the rest. He exhibited confusion about every problem except the first one, including item c, for which he indicated 9 = 9 18. He was not yet ready to take on these ideas. The teacher recorded his explanations and reactions on his paper. He commented, "It's not right" or "It doesn't make sense" without giving any explanation.

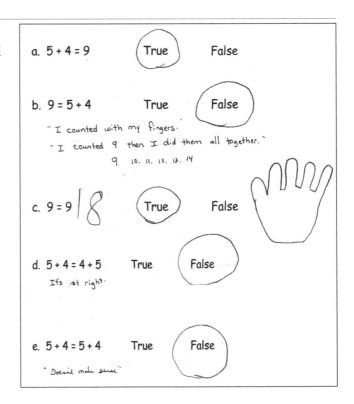

a. 5 + 4 = 9   (True)   False

b. 9 = 5 + 4   True   (False)
"I counted with my fingers."
"I counted 9 then I did them all together."
9 10. 11. 12. 13. 14

c. 9 = 9 | 8   (True)   False

d. 5 + 4 = 4 + 5   True   (False)
It's not right.

e. 5 + 4 = 5 + 4   True   (False)
"Doesn't make sense."

Cheryl: Beginning Understanding

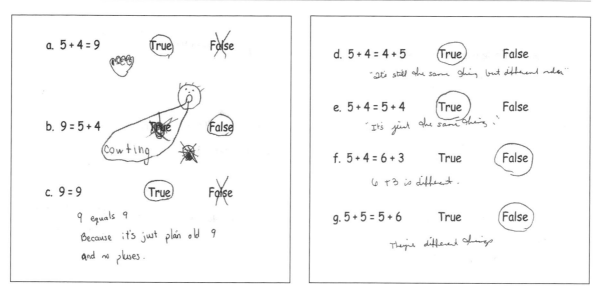

Cheryl's work shows that she considered each problem carefully and then made a determination of true or false. She accepted that $9 = 9$ was true because "9 equals 9" but was not sure about $9 = 5 + 4$, which she said was false. She identified $5 + 4 = 4 + 5$ and $5 + 4 = 5 + 4$ as true because they have the same numbers on both sides. However, she reasoned similarly as she marked as false both $5 + 4 = 6 + 3$ and $5 + 5 = 5 + 6$ because the numbers are not the same on both sides.

Savanna: On Target

Savanna stated, "All but the last (problem) is true." She had difficulty writing out her reasoning, so she dictated it to the teacher to record. For $9 = 9$, Savanna told her teacher, "That's easy. It's the same numbers, nine is the same as nine." She reasoned that the three expressions $5 + 4 = 4 + 5$, $5 + 4 = 5 + 4$, and $5 + 4 = 6 + 3$ were all true because each side "had the same amount, nine."

Lenny Going Beyond

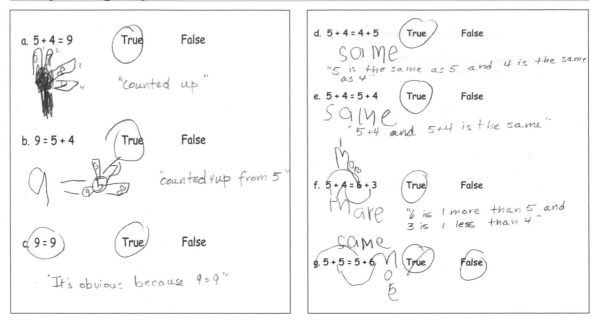

Lenny had a clear understanding of the equals sign as showing a balance of the quantities on each side of it. The notes added by the teacher reveal a level of sophistication as Lenny thought through each problem. He was often able to determine whether a statement was true or false without carrying out the computations.

Variations for the Range of Learners

* Present fewer number sentences, present them one at a time, or present the first three number sentences on one day and the others on another day.
* Eliminate the last number sentence, and focus only on the ones that are true.
* Include more numbers, including 0, in some of the number sentences.
* Use larger numbers, or use number sentences having the same structures but employing other operations.

Geometry

YOUNG children begin forming concepts of shape long before they receive any formal schooling. They tend to recognize and describe objects by appearance or by qualities, so we commonly hear a young child refer to the "pointy" shape or the shape that "looks like a door." Children's informal understanding of geometry should be expanded through explorations, investigations, and discussions of shapes and structures. Students can compare and sort building blocks as they put them away at the end of play time, for instance, by identifying their similarities and differences. They can use commonly available materials, such as cereal boxes, to explore attributes of shapes, or use folded paper to investigate symmetry and congruence. They can create shapes on geoboards or dot paper and represent those shapes in drawings and block constructions. They should also be engaged in combining or cutting apart shapes to form new shapes (NCTM 2000). The study of geometry gives students opportunities to explore, describe, analyze, and investigate relationships among figures, structures, and the surrounding environment. Additionally, students' understanding of geometry and spatial reasoning lays a foundation for learning other mathematics topics.

The focus of geometry at the early grades should be on helping students explore shapes, their attributes, and spatial relationships. Spatial sense is described as "insights and intuitions about two- and three-dimensional shapes and their characteristics, the interrelationships of shapes, and the effects of changes to shapes" (NCTM 1989, p. 48). To help students develop spatial sense and geometric reasoning, young children need to be actively engaged in exploring their environment and investigating problems using concrete materials as illustrated in the activities in *Navigating through Geometry in Prekindergarten–Grade 2* (Findell, Small, Cavanagh, Dacey, Greenes, and Sheffield 2001) The assessment tasks in this chapter are linked with the kinds of experiences that research suggests students should be engaged in doing (Crowley 1987). The tasks can be used to assess a wide range of spatial and geometric understandings.

Geometry Assessment Items

Standard: Specify locations and describe spatial relationships using coordinate geometry and other representational systems

Expectation: Describe, name, and interpret relative positions in space and apply ideas about relative position

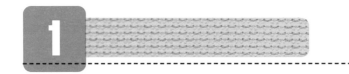

I Spy: Locating Objects in Our Classroom

Grade range: Pre-K–K

About the mathematics: An awareness of the location of items in relation to one another is important for young children to develop. In the "I Spy" task, students are asked to identify objects in their classroom on the basis of the positional directions given. When the teacher asks, "I spy something above the door. What do you think I see?" the student needs to correctly interpret the words used, consider his or her position relative to the information provided, and identify the correct object. Those students who successfully identify the object demonstrate an understanding of location and of the vocabulary used to describe relative position of objects in space.

TASK

Let's play the "I Spy" game. I am going to describe a place in our classroom where I see a particular object. Your job is to tell me what object I see. For example, if I say, "I spy something on the table. What do you think it might be?" I might be referring to the book that is on the table.

"I spy something (<u>insert positional word</u>) the (<u>insert location</u>)."

Use of variety of positional words, such as *front, back, above, below, between, next, top, bottom, same side, different side, on, over,* and *inside.* Examples include "I spy something over the door," "I spy something under the table," and "I spy something next to the sink."

Using this assessment task: Working individually with a student, ask three or four different questions to determine whether the student understands a variety of positional terms. A helpful approach is to prepare a list of positional words ahead of time, along with a few ideas of locations in the classroom to use for the task. Remember, the task is not to stump the child but to gain an awareness of her or his understanding of locations and positional terms. Select locations that the student can easily see from where she or he is seated. Selecting locations that have more than one possible answer may be more challenging for students. Choosing a location that has more than one possible answer also means that the teacher must be very specific in describing the position of the object. Using a location with more than one possible answer has the added benefit of allowing the teacher to gain more insight into a student's reasoning.

Solution: An appropriate solution is one in which a student correctly names an object in the described position, not necessarily the specific object the teacher had in mind.

Continuum of Understanding

Limited Understanding

Provides no response or no appropriate response, or names random objects in the classroom having no connection with the positional statements

Developing Understanding

May be familiar with and able to use some positional words but may not yet have learned others or may consistently misuse them; for example, may be able to work with the words *front* and *back* but be unable to identify objects for the term *between*

Strong Understanding

Successfully identifies an object that meets the criteria stipulated

Looking for Evidence of Understanding

The teacher made anecdotal records of students' responses. The following students were interviewed and were given three different prompts: "I spy something near the door," "I spy something on the table," and "I spy something between the dolls on the shelf."

Mark: Developing Understanding

Mark correctly named something near the door and on the table but gave no response to the items that involved the word *between*. Mark's responses reveal that he is on his way to understanding, but he needs more experiences with addressing the concept of *between*.

Mia and Maria: Strong Understanding

Mia demonstrated her understanding by either pointing to, or walking over to, the object located in the described position; she did not express her knowledge verbally. Maria gave multiple solutions for "near the door," saying, "Lots of things are near the door…." She identified all three items on the table and added, "The pencil is near the book. The block is not." She also correctly identified something between the dolls on the shelf. Mia and Maria both appeared to have complete understanding of the situation. Maria's additional comments lend insight into her ability to verbalize her understanding.

Variations for the Range of Learners

- *Focus on a particular positional word.* Rather than focus on the range of positional words, the task can be used to assess students' understanding of a particular word; for example, the teacher might ask students to identify three things that are above another object. Possible student responses might include "The book is on the shelf" and "My pencil is on top of my desk."

- *Ask the student to place a certain object in a particular location.* Receptive language often develops before expressive language. In this version of the task, the student is asked to demonstrate understanding by acting out the situation by pointing to or placing a specified object correctly, for example, "Place the teddy bear above the book" or "Place the green pattern block in front of your nose."

- *Using multiple positional words.* Using more than one positional phrase in the description can increase the complexity of this task. For example, the teacher might say, "I spy something that is under the table and next to the pencil." In such a situation, the student must consider the relative position of the object on the basis of multiple factors.

Standard: Use visualization, spatial reasoning, and geometric modeling to solve problems

Expectations

- Create mental images of geometric shapes using spatial memory and spatial visualization
- Create representations as a record of spatial reasoning

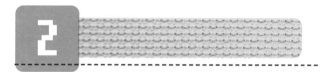

Quick Images of Shapes

Grade range: Pre-K–2

About the mathematics: Spatial visualization is the ability to comprehend visual information and imagine the relationships and movements of objects in two- and three-dimensional space. This task fosters insight into students' spatial memory and spatial visualization by examining their ability to relate the component parts and orientations of geometric designs.

TASK

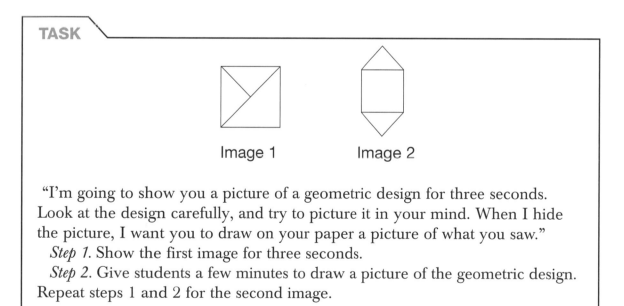

Image 1   Image 2

"I'm going to show you a picture of a geometric design for three seconds. Look at the design carefully, and try to picture it in your mind. When I hide the picture, I want you to draw on your paper a picture of what you saw."

Step 1. Show the first image for three seconds.

Step 2. Give students a few minutes to draw a picture of the geometric design. Repeat steps 1 and 2 for the second image.

Source: Adapted from *From Paces to Feet: Measuring and Data,* by Karen Economopoulos, Jan Mokros, and Susan Jo Russell (Palo Alto, Calif.: Dale Seymour Publications, 1999).

Using this assessment task: Prepare a transparency of the "Quick Images of Shapes" blackline master, or draw each image on chart paper. To ensure the success of this task, be sure to reveal only one image at a time. Each student needs a blank piece of paper and a pencil. This task is designed for whole-class administration. Be sure that all students are seated so that they have a clear view of the overhead screen or chart paper. In a follow-up discussion, ask students, "What did you see? How did you decide what to draw?"

Solution: An appropriate response resembles the image shown here. The drawing should be in the same orientation as the original and should preserve the same relationships among the component parts.

Continuum of Understanding

Limited Understanding

Produces either no response or drawings that show very little resemblance to the original designs

Developing Understanding

Draws images that show some resemblance to the original designs, but the relationships among, and orientation of, some of the component parts do not match those in the original images

Strong Understanding

Makes accurate drawings of both images; the relationships and orientation of the component parts match those of the original geometric designs

Looking for Evidence of Understanding

This task was given to a group of first-grade students. The teacher analyzed the images and separated them into three piles–limited, developing, or strong understanding.

Ralph and Lisa: Developing Understanding

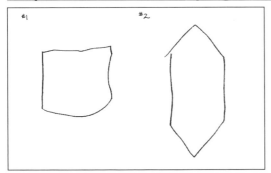

Ralph

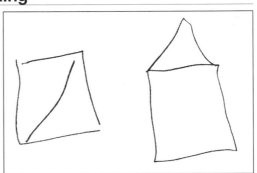

Lisa

Both Ralph's and Lisa's work revealed that they were developing an understanding of spatial visualization. Each of the figures they produced resembled the image shown; however, essential features of the images were missing. In his sketch, Ralph failed to include the line segments that appear in the interior of the figure. In contrast, Lisa realized that the figure included interior line segments, but she either did not include them all or drew a partially complete figure.

Pedro: Strong Understanding

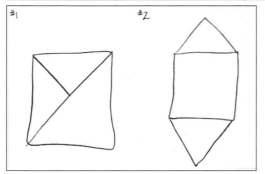

Pedro's sketches indicated that he captured all the components of the figures.

Variations for the Range of Learners

- Allow more time. Show each image for another three seconds, and allow students to revise their drawings.
- Simplify the design. Use simpler designs to lower the difficulty of the task.

- Use more complex designs. Increase the difficulty off the task by using more complex designs.

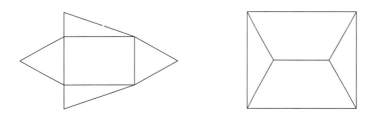

Standard: Analyze characteristics and properties of two and three-dimensional geometric shapes and develop a mathematical argument about geometric relationships

Expectation: Recognize, name, build, draw, compare, and sort two- and three-dimensional objects

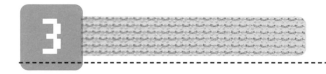

Can You Build What I Build?

Grade range: Pre-K–2

About the mathematics: The "Can You Build What I Build?" task gives the teacher an opportunity to assess whether students can identify spatial relationships between objects as they work toward building a similar structure. By examining the students' structures, teachers can identify which students need more such experiences to develop their spatial sense.

TASK

"I'm going to build a design with the pattern blocks. Once I'm done, I want you to use your pattern blocks to build a design just like mine."

Build one of the following structures or a structure of your own design for the students to duplicate.

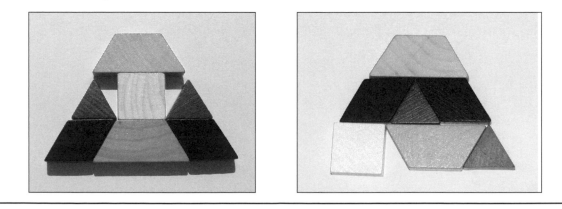

Using this assessment task: This task can be used with individual students or small groups. It can also be used with a whole class if the design is built with overhead pattern blocks on a projector. Students need patterns blocks to build the modeled structure. Place a small set of pattern blocks in a basket from which the students may choose which blocks they need to build the design. Be sure to note not only the final structure that students build but also the way they approach the task. Do they readily build the structure accurately, or do they struggle to place the blocks in the appropriate positions?

Solution: The structure created by the students should be identical to the one made by the teacher.

Continuum of Understanding

Limited Understanding

Struggles to build the structure, frequently adjusting and rearranging the blocks; possibly uses the correct blocks, but creates a final structure that does not resemble the one modeled by the teacher

Developing Understanding

Needs to adjust his or her structure several times in the building process; includes some of the features of the model at each iteration of his or her structure, but is not completely accurate in replicating it; places some of the blocks in the wrong places, orients a particular shape differently from the original, or orients the entire figure differently from the original

Strong Understanding

Accurately builds the structure with very little or no revision during the building process

Looking for Evidence of Understanding

Nadia: Limited Understanding

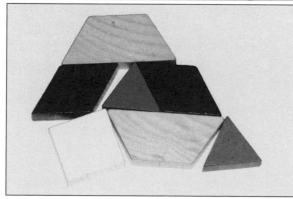

Nadia first struggled to pick out the appropriate pattern blocks. She had to double-check and adjust her choices a few times before she had used the correct blocks. Arranging the blocks to replicate the original structure was a challenge for her. The picture shows one of her attempts.

Luis: Developing Understanding

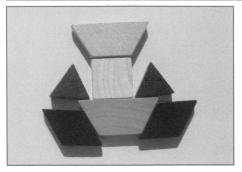

Luis compared his structure with the original and realized that he had to turn the top trapezoid around. He pushed the rhombi and triangles together until they were adjacent, but he did not realize that they were in the wrong orientation.

Jamecyn: Strong Understanding

Jamecyn quickly built her structure. When she compared it with the original, she immediately realized that it needed to be adjusted. She quickly made the adjustment to create an accurate structure.

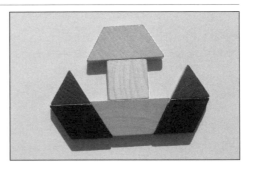

Variations for the Range of Learners

The complexity of this task can be reduced or increased by altering the structures that are presented to students.

- To simplify the task, decrease the number of different shapes that are used to make the original structure.
- Another way to simplify the task is to present a structure that resembles a familiar object; for example, build the structure at the right, which looks like a tree.
- Using more-complex shapes can increase the difficulty of the task. For example, asking students to replicate the structure below adds a level of complexity to the task.

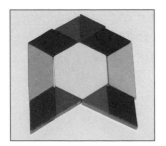

Standard: Analyze characteristics and properties of two- and three- dimensional geometric shapes and develop mathematical arguments about geometric relationships

Expectations

- Recognize and name two-dimensional shapes
- Describe attributes and parts of two-dimensional figures

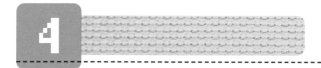

All about Triangles

Grade range: K–2

About the mathematics: The "All about Triangles" task requires students to compare and contrast geometric figures to determine similarities and differences among them. The intent of this task is to tease out the differences between student's superficial and complete understanding of triangles. For example, a student with complete understanding recognizes a triangle no matter what its orientation or the length of its sides.

TASK

Mark all the triangles on the page.
Tell how you know that they are triangles.

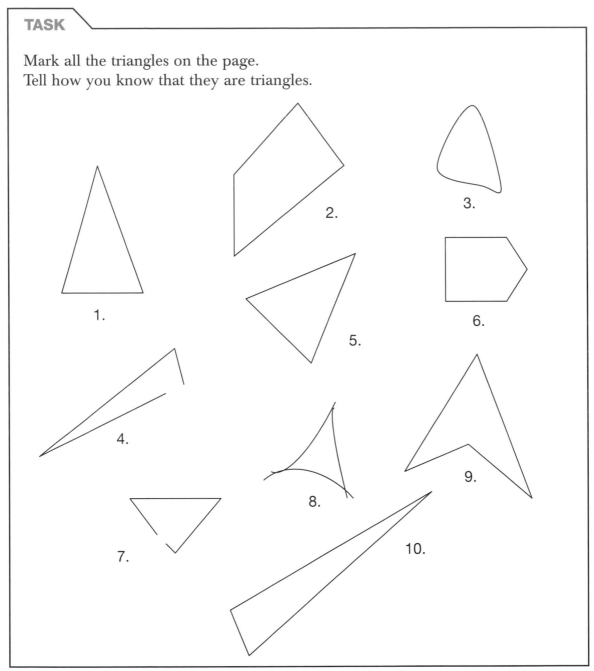

Inspired by "Identifying triangles" task in the article titled "Geometry" by William F. Burger in *Arithmetic Teacher*, vol. 32, no. 6, pp. 52–56.

Using this assessment task: This task is designed to be used during individual student interviews. Prepare a copy of the "All about Triangles" blackline master for each student. When the student identifies a given figure as a triangle, important information about her or his understanding is gleaned by asking, "What makes you think that is a triangle?" or "How do you know that is a triangle?"

Solution

Figures 1, 5, and 10 are triangles because they are all closed figures, made up of exactly three line segments.

Figure 2 is not a triangle, because it has four sides.

Figure 3 is not a triangle, because it is made up of curves.

Figure 4 is not a triangle, because it is not a closed figure.

Figure 6 is not a triangle, because it has more than three sides.

Figure 7 is not a triangle, because it is not a closed figure.

Figure 8 is not a triangle, because it is made with curves.

Figure 9 is not a triangle, because it has four sides.

Continuum of Understanding

Limited Understanding

Is inconsistent in his or her use of particular characteristics to determine whether a figure is a triangle

Developing Understanding

Identifies all figures that appear to have three sides; may include some items that are not triangles but that have some of the characteristics of a triangle

Strong Understanding

Recognizes all the shapes that are triangles; may use informal language to give an accurate definition of a triangle, for example, state that a triangle has only three sides; that it has three corners, or angles; and that its sides meet, or are closed

Looking for Evidence of Understanding

In administering this task, a first-grade teacher learned that all of her students demonstrated some knowledge about triangles but that their understanding was limited. Many students included some of the figures that are not triangles. Many students did not understand that triangles do not have curved sides. Some students also included figures that were not closed, particularly shapes 4 and 7. The teacher remarked, "Lots of children included number 7. I think this is because the break in the line is very small. Next time I would make it bigger. Some of the children also said that [shape 7] was an 'upside down' triangle." A few students did not include shape 10, stating that it was "too skinny" to be a triangle.

Manny: Limited Understanding

Manny's statement reveals that he had a limited understanding of triangles. He focused on the number of "points," or angles. He apparently did not realize that the sides of a triangle must be line segments.

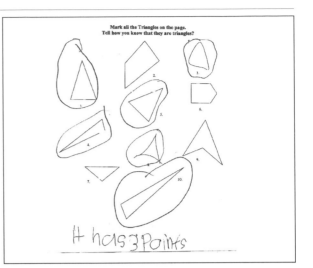

Tina and Andrew: Developing Understanding

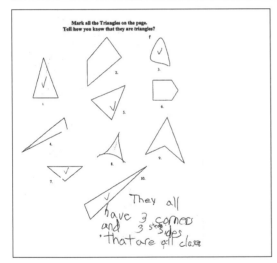

Tina

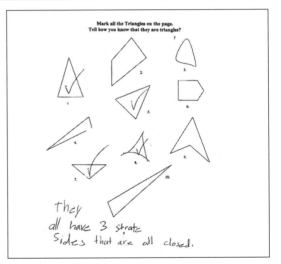

Andrew

Tina and Andrew gave similar definitions for a triangle. Although they both stated that a triangle must be closed, they both identified shape 7 as a triangle. They may have selected that shape because the break in its side was rather small. Both students noted that the sides should be straight, but each included a figure with curved sides. These two students may not have understood what having straight sides means in the context of a triangle.

Camille: Strong Understanding

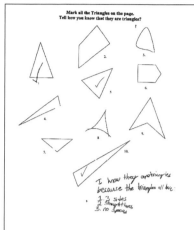

Camille demonstrated a strong understanding of triangles by correctly identifying the triangles and by stating three characteristics of a triangle.

Variations for the Range of Learners

- *Drawing triangles.* Vary the task by asking students to draw different triangles. For example, first ask students to draw a triangle; then ask them to draw a different triangle and to state how it is different from the first. Possibly continue this sort of dialogue until the student exhausts the possible variations that he or she can create. When giving instructions, emphasize that size is not the only thing that makes triangles different.

- *Sort figures.* Ask students to sort the triangles according to one or more of their attributes. Ahead of time, draw or cut and paste each of the figures onto a card. Instruct each student to sort the set of cards. The student should decide on the criteria being used to sort the figures and should be required to identify the criteria that he or she chose for the sorting process. The sorting activity lends insight into how the student is thinking about the attributes of a triangle.

Standard: Analyze characteristics and properties of two- and three- dimensional geometric shapes and develop mathematical arguments about geometric relationships

Expectation: Compare and describe the attributes of two-dimensional shapes

What's in Common?

Grade range: 1–2

About the mathematics: The intent of the "What's in Common?" task is to ascertain whether students are able to compare examples and nonexamples to determine the characteristics of a set of shapes. This task lends insights into students' ability to recognize similarities and differences of triangles and into their use of language or terminology to describe the attributes of triangles.

TASK

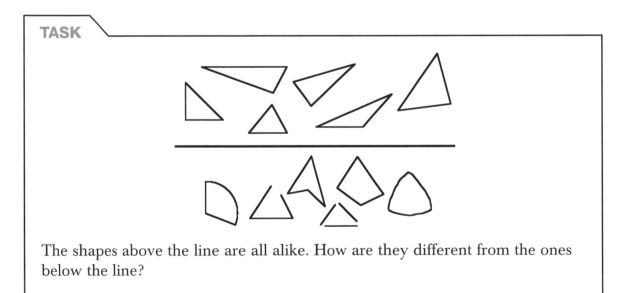

The shapes above the line are all alike. How are they different from the ones below the line?

Source: *Principles and Standards for School Mathematics* (Reston, Va.: National Council of Teachers of Mathematics [NCTM], 2000, p. 98).

Using this assessment task: This task is designed to be used with individual students, small groups, or the whole class. Make one copy of the "Comparing Shapes" blackline master for each student. Be sure to remind the students that the figures above the line are all alike in some way. The goal of the activity is for students to examine the characteristics of the shapes to find commonalities among the shapes above the line that distinguish them from the shapes below the line. Teachers have found that preparing an anecdotal recording sheet like the one below is helpful for recording the students' reasoning.

Student name:		Date:	
	Yes	No	Comments
Says the figures are closed.			
Indicates that the figures above the line are all triangles.			
Recognizes that each figure above the line has exactly three sides (and/or three corners/angles).			
Indicates that figures with curves are not triangles.			
Shows an awareness that figures need to be closed.			

Solution: The shapes above the lines are all triangles. Each one is a closed shape with three sides and three angles. The shapes below the line are not triangles, because of one or more of the following reasons:

- The figure is not closed.
- The figure includes a curve.
- The figure has more than three sides.

Continuum of Understanding

Limited Evidence

May state that the figures above the line are triangles but not be able to identify the attributes that make them so; may indicate that some of the figures above the line are not triangles

Adequate Evidence

Identifies some characteristics common to the shapes above the line that distinguish them from some of the shapes below the line

Strong Evidence

Recognizes all the shapes above the line as triangles, describes why each of the items is a triangle, and articulates why the shapes below the line are not triangles

Looking for Evidence of Understanding

Rebecca: Limited Evidence

Student name _Rebecca_

	Yes	No	Comments
Says the figures are closed		✓	"They don't all look like triangles. Some look are too pointy but they have 3 sides."
Indicates that the figures above the line are all triangles		✓	
Recognized that each figure above the line has exactly 3 sides (and/or 3 corners)	✓		
Indicates that figures with curves are not triangles		✓	"Some of these look like triangles, but they don't touch all the way."
Shows an awareness that figures need to be closed.	✓		

Rebecca realized that the shapes above the line have three sides, but she was not sure whether they are all triangles.

Paul: Adequate Evidence

Student name _Paul_

	Yes	No	Comments
Says the figures are closed		✓	"I know these are triangles they have 3 sides and 3 corners. They have 3 points too."
Indicates that the figures above the line are all triangles	✓		
Recognized that each figure above the line has exactly 3 sides (and/or 3 corners)	✓		"Some of these look round and don't touch."
Indicates that figures with curves are not triangles	✓		
Shows an awareness that figures need to be closed.	✓		"They don't look like triangles. Well, sort of but they aren't."

Paul seemed to focus on each set of shapes separately. He identified the shapes above the line as triangles but then had difficulty distinguishing those shapes from the shapes below the line.

Tasha: Strong Evidence

Student name   *Tasha*

	Yes	No	Comments
Says the figures are closed	✓		"These all touch at the points, but some of these don't"
Indicates that the figures above the line are all triangles	✓		
Recognized that each figure above the line has exactly 3 sides (and/or 3 corners)	✓		"A triangle has 3 sides and 3 corners. Some of these don't"
Indicates that figures with curves are not triangles	✓		
Shows an awareness that figures need to be closed.	✓		"Some bend, they aren't straight."

Tasha made several correct statements that distinguished the set of shapes above the line from the set of shapes below the line.

Variations for the Range of Learners

- *Decrease the number of examples*. Decreasing the number of examples may help students focus on the characteristics of the shapes without being overwhelmed by the number of shapes they are asked to examine.
- *Use different shapes*. Modify this task to help students examine features of other geometric shapes. For example, present students with examples and non-examples of two-dimensional shapes (e.g., rectangles) or three-dimensional objects.
- *Focus on one particular characteristic*. Focus on triangles, for example, and elect to show nonexamples that are not closed figures. The intent would be for students to see that triangles are closed figures. In a different activity, emphasize another characteristic by providing nonexamples that are all curved figures or that all have more than three sides.

Standard: Specify locations and describe spatial relationships using coordinate geometry and other representational systems

Expectations

- Describe, name, and interpret relative position in space and apply ideas about relative position
- Find and name locations with simple relationships such as "near to" and in coordinate systems such as maps

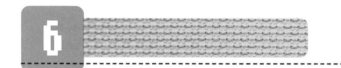

Visiting a Friend

Grade range: 1–2

About the mathematics: The "Visiting a Friend" task uses a coordinate grid to foster insights into students' spatial understandings of navigation and maps. The activity asks students to determine various paths to go from one point to another on a grid. This task yields information about students' understanding of directions, distance, and position in space. In completing this task, students are expected to use such directional phrases as up and down and right and left, along with concepts of distance, by counting the number of spaces traveled. It also lends insight into students' use of coordinates to name positions.

TASK

The streets in Squareville are numbered 0 to 10 and run left to right. The avenues are also numbered 0 to 10 and run from bottom to top.

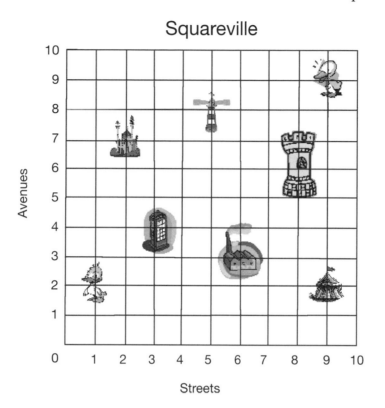

1. Give Mr. Duck directions that he can follow to go to Mr. Quack. Mr. Duck is at location (1, 2), and Mr. Quack is at location (9, 9).

2. Describe another way for Mr. Duck to go to Mr. Quack.

Using this assessment task: This task is designed to be used in an individual interview with a student. Give the student a copy of the "Squareville" blackline master and several markers of different colors. The markers allow students to identify and color-code more than one path on the same map. To begin, ask the student to use a marker to draw a path from Mr. Duck to Mr. Quack. Explain to the student that he or she must travel along the lines that represent streets and avenues in the city and must go around the obstacles (e.g., factory, tent). Ask the student to describe the path taken. Assess the language the student uses to distinguish among navigational ideas, such as direction (which way?), distance (how far?), and position (where?). Ask the student to identify a different path that Mr. Quack could take to go to Mr. Duck. This challenge increases the opportunity for students to use different directional and positional phrases and to demonstrate flexibility in reasoning through the task.

Solution: A correct answer shows a path that moves along the line segments without crossing any of the obstacles. Many correct solutions are possible. Students should use appropriate directions, distances, or coordinate positions to describe the movement along a particular path. For example, one correct response is "Mr. Duck needs to go right 4 spaces, up 5 spaces, right 2 spaces, up 2 more spaces, and right 2 spaces to arrive at Mr. Quack."

Continuum of Understanding

Initial Understanding

Points to a path that could be taken, but does not describe the path using directional phrases or distances

Developing Understanding

Attempts to describe a path using informal language and distances but has difficulty identifying appropriate directional phrases, for example, may say, "You have to go this way [pointing to the right] three spaces and then this way [pointing up] four."

Strong Understanding

Describes direction and distance for multiple paths; uses such directional terminology as *right-left* and *up-down* to describe paths that can be taken; determines correct distances, and uses coordinates accurately

Looking for Evidence of Understanding

Several teachers who administered this task reported that younger students were not likely to use the terminology *right* or *left* until prompted. The teachers did discover that most students could point to and describe the chosen paths by using familiar terminology, and that some students attempted to describe coordinate positions by using street or avenue names.

Tyrek: Initial Understanding

Tyrek simply said, "Just go up and over." When asked to find another path, he continued to describe it in general terms of "going up" and "going over."

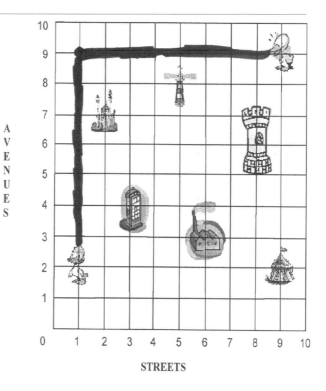

Morgan: Developing Understanding

Morgan's paths were a bit more complex. Once prompted, she tried to describe directions using *right* and *left*. She also used some street names and some distances but did so inconsistently. For the path shown, she explained, "Mr. Duck starts on 2 Avenue and goes to 5 Street. Then up 3 squares. Then straight across right to 10 Street. Then up to 9 Street [meaning Avenue] and goes back 1 square to Mr. Quack."

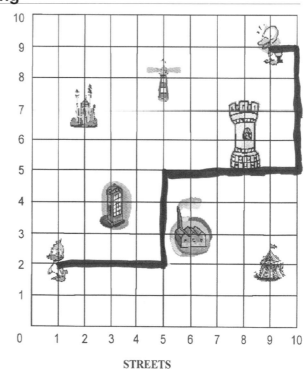

Veronica: Strong Understanding

Veronica placed a dot at each location as she described the path that should be taken. She said, "Go to (5, 2), then go up to (5, 5), then go to (7, 5), then go to (7, 9), then go to (9, 9) and you are there." When asked to identify a different way, she said, "Go to (4, 2), then to (4, 4), then go to (9, 4), and then to (9, 9) and you are there."

Variations for the Range of Learners

- *Use fewer obstacles.* Decreasing the amount of visual input that students must address may give them more opportunities to focus on and describe a path. An example of such a task is the "Going to School" activity found in NCTM's *Navigating through Geometry in Prekindergarten–Grade 2* (Findell et al. 2001).

- *Ask for directions step-by-step.* The movements toward a particular object can be separated into a series of steps that emphasize a particular directional word. For example, the following is a series of questions that can be posed for Squareville: "What direction should Mr. Duck walk in order to get to the tent?" "What would Mr. Duck do if he wanted to get to the factory?" "How can he get from the factory to the lighthouse?"

Standard: Apply transformation and use symmetry to analyze mathematical situations

Expectation: Recognize and create shapes that have symmetry

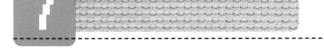

Cookie Pattern Symmetry

Grade range: 1–2

About the mathematics: The "Cookie Pattern Symmetry" task is designed to gain insight into students' understanding of line symmetry. A figure has line symmetry if the figure can be folded along a line so that the two resulting parts match exactly.

TASK

Aunt Sally's Cookies

Aunt Sally likes to make interesting shaped cookies for her nephews Billy and Bob. To get a cookie, they have to tell her how to make one cut in the cookie so that they each get a fair share. Show Aunt Sally how to cut each cookie into two pieces that are the exact same size and shape. Billy will receive one piece and Bob will receive one piece.

Could Aunt Sally cut any of the cookies in more than one way?
If so, explain how.

Using this assessment task: This task is designed for use with individual students, small groups, or the whole class. Make one copy of the "Aunt Sally's Cookies" blackline master for each student. Give students a tool that is thin and straight, such as a coffee stirrer, a piece of spaghetti, or even a piece of string. Encourage students to explore how they could "cut" the cookie before they actually mark the lines of symmetry on the figures on their papers. Ask the students how they can determine whether Billy and Bob are getting exact, same-sized cookie halves. Possibly encourage students to use cutouts of the cookie shapes that they can fold, or guide them to use a mirror to determine whether the "cuts" they think divide the cookies in half really are going to result in halves.

Solution: The lines of symmetry of the shapes are shown below. Three of the shapes have more than one line of symmetry.

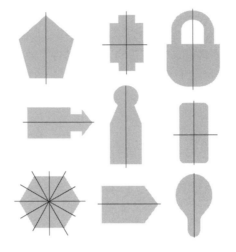

Continuum of Understanding

Limited Understanding

Divides some shapes into two or more parts, and may attempt to create fair shares from the pieces; does not draw a line of symmetry

Developing Understanding

Has difficulty finding the precise line of symmetry on a shape, but provides evidence of knowing that both pieces should match exactly; may identify one line of symmetry in most figures but does not acknowledge that some figures have more than one line of symmetry

Strong Understanding

Not only finds one line of symmetry but discerns which shapes have more than one line of symmetry and which shapes cannot have more than one line of symmetry

Looking for Evidence of Understanding

In administering this task, all students were able to visualize and draw a line that was close to the line of symmetry for some of the simpler figures. No student was able to indicate all the lines of symmetry for the hexagon.

Joey: Limited Understanding

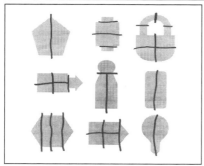

Joey cut some of the cookies into more than two parts. He focused on being fair to Billy and Bob. For some of the cookies, he said he would give the extra piece to Aunt Sally.

Nakeia: Developing Understanding

Nakeia commented that you "usually just have to go straight down" and that "sometimes you need to go across." She seemed perplexed when asked whether the cookies could be cut in more than one way, and replied that they were already cut.

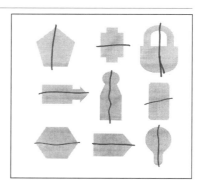

Jenna: Developing Understanding

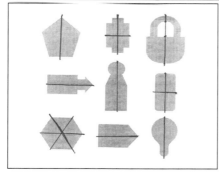

Jenna folded the paper, held it up to the light for each shape, and used a ruler to carefully draw the lines. She immediately realized that some of the shapes have more than one line of symmetry.

Variations for the Range of Learners

- *Decrease the complexity of the shapes.* Use shapes with just one obvious line of symmetry to focus students' attention.
- *Use shapes with multiple lines of symmetry.* Use shapes with more than one line of symmetry to determine students' level of sophistication regarding the concept of symmetry.

Standard: Apply transformation and use symmetry to analyze mathematical situations

Expectation: Recognize and apply slides, flips, and turns

Shapes in Motion

Grade level: 1–2

About the mathematics: A transformation is the result of the effect of motion on an object. In the "Shapes in Motion" task, students explore three common transformations—translations (slides), rotations (turns), and reflections (flips), which change an object's position or orientation but not its size or shape. The study of transformations is an important part of spatial learning.

TASK

Color in and then cut out these shapes:

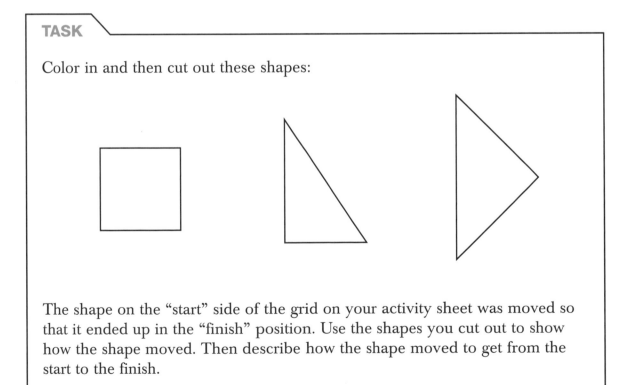

The shape on the "start" side of the grid on your activity sheet was moved so that it ended up in the "finish" position. Use the shapes you cut out to show how the shape moved. Then describe how the shape moved to get from the start to the finish.

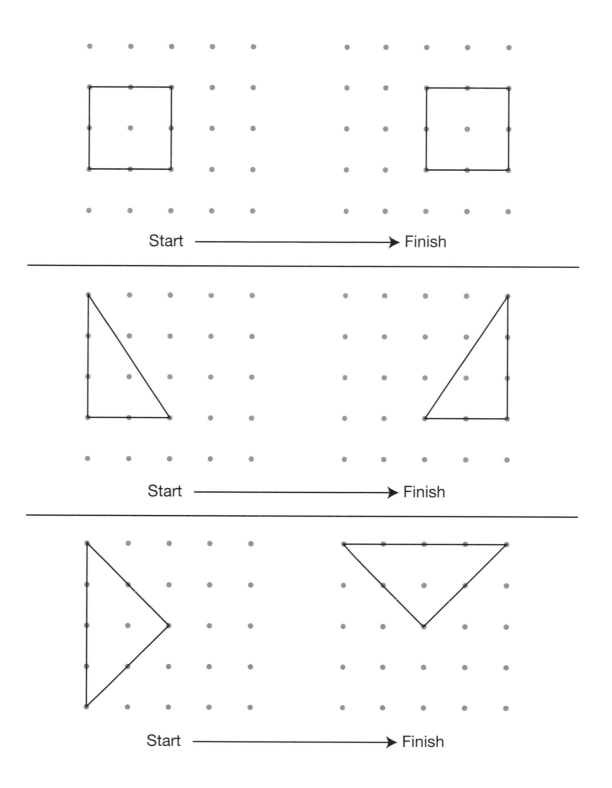

Start ⟶ Finish

Start ⟶ Finish

Start ⟶ Finish

Using this assessment task: This task is designed to be used during individual interviews with students. Make a copy of the "Shapes in Motion" blackline master for each student. The goal of the activity is to learn whether students can determine the motion required to take the shape from the "start" position to the "finish" position. Students need to consider the shape in its totality to be successful with the task. Have students place the cutout shape on the start position and then investigate how it might have moved to be in the finish position. The use of the Geoboard is not recommended, because the student may focus on the placement of the rubber bands without examining the effect on the entire shape.

Solution

Square. The motion is a slide or reflection (flip).
Right triangle. The motion is a reflection (flip).
Isosceles triangle. The motion is a rotation (turn).

Continuum of Understanding

Initial Understanding

Indicates that some motion is involved but is unable to demonstrate or articulate a specific type of motion

Developing Understanding

Demonstrates what occurs for some of the shapes, but needs to use trial and error to replicate the transformation; may use inappropriate terminology to describe the motion

Strong Understanding

Readily recognizes a single movement, and uses appropriate terminology to describe the motion

Looking for Evidence of Understanding

Although this task was designed to be used in an interview situation, first- and second-grade teachers thought that their students could do it on their own. Accordingly, they presented the task as a whole-class assessment and asked students to write out a description of how the shape was moved. If a student was not successful, the teachers followed up with an interview during which they asked the student to talk about the observations that he or she made. Many students used informal language to correctly identify the movements.

Theresa: Initial Understanding

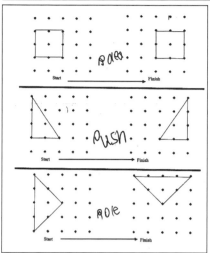

A follow-up interview with Theresa revealed that she could not identify specific movements for the shapes but had used trial and error to place the cutout shapes on the finished positions. She described some of the movements as "rolling" and "pushing."

Loyola and Shawn: Developing Understanding

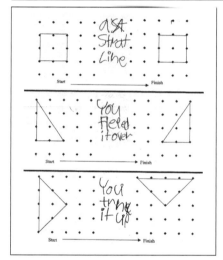

Loyola

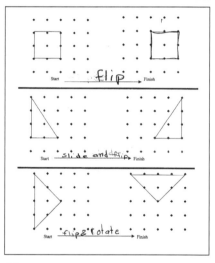

Shawn

Students with developing understanding, such as Loyola, identified a specific movement but had difficulty explaining it. In a follow-up interview she demonstrated a slide and explained that for the square, "you just move it over in a straight line." For the isosceles triangle, she said as she rotated it that you "turn it up." She showed and stated that the right triangle was flipped. Other students, such as Shawn, reported that two movements were necessary to get to the finished position, particularly for the triangles. For the right triangle, he explained, "You slide it over to the end and then flip it around."

Karen: Strong Understanding

Karen readily visualized and described the transformations without the use of the cutout shapes. She first wrote "move" for the square and then remembered that this movement was called a slide.

Variations for the Range of Learners

- *Remove the grid.* Simplify the task by posing it to students without the image of a geoboard grid, thereby encouraging them to focus on the movement of the shape rather than on the geoboard pegs as an indicator of what has occurred.
- *Perform specific motions.* Give students a particular shape or object to work with (e.g., preferably a shape with a distinguishable characteristic, such as a concave pentagon), and ask them to perform a particular motion. For example, ask, "How would the figure appear if you flipped it? Turned it to the left? Slid it over?"

Measurement

YOUNG children's curiosity is evident to anyone who watches how children engage with their environment. Young children continually make comparisons between and among objects with which they interact. They test to see which item is longer or shorter, which cup is taller or shorter, which truck goes faster or slower, which rock is heavier or lighter, which box is larger, which ball is bigger, who dug a deeper hole, or who has more stickers. Such informal measurement activities, as well as more structured measurement experiences, can simultaneously teach important everyday skills and develop measurement concepts and processes that will be formalized and expanded in later years.

In the prekindergarten through second-grade (Pre-K–2) years, children begin to develop an understanding of attributes by looking at, touching, or directly comparing objects. They use calendars and clocks to determine elapsed time; and they explore order relationships by comparing multiple objects, such as a baseball, a soccer ball, and a plastic golf ball. They use the language of measurement to indicate that in a collection of three balls, the golf ball is the smallest, the baseball is smaller than the soccer ball but larger than the golf ball, and the soccer ball is the largest. They use such words as *longer, taller, shorter, bigger, smaller, heavier, lighter,* and *deeper.*

Measurement is one of the most widely used applications of mathematics, and helps students connect ideas within areas of mathematics and between mathematics and other disciplines. In grades pre-K–2, measurement activities can teach important everyday skills, strengthen mathematical knowledge, build understanding, and further children's mathematical thinking. The fact that children's conceptual understanding of measurement is highly influenced by consistent experiences in the early grades is well documented. Students in those grades should become acquainted with the use of simple measuring tools and engage in activities that involve making comparisons and estimating measurements.

Teaching measurement to young children involves providing them with ample hands-on experiences that involve concrete objects and measuring instruments. Although much of the measurement that is done during the early grades is linear, young children actively engage in examining volume as they pour sand or water

117

from one container to another. They engage in making conjectures about the amount of water or sand that a particular container can hold. Young children are also fascinated by weighing items. They enjoy predicting which object is heavier, which two objects might weigh the same, or what will happen if they put three cubes on one side of a pan balance and twenty-five links on the other side.

This chapter presents tasks for assessing children's conceptual and procedural understanding of measuring using several different attributes. We hope that the measurement tasks will yield valuable information about students' developmental growth and be a tool that pre-K–2 teachers can use to monitor students' progress and make further instructional decisions. All educators should keep in mind the essential point that assessment should not merely be done *to* students; rather, it should be done *for* students, to guide and enhance their learning (NCTM 2000). Assessment tasks can become a routine part of the ongoing classroom activity rather than an interruption. Although assessment is used for a variety of reasons, its main goal is to advance students' learning and inform teachers as they make instructional decisions (NCTM 1995).

Measurement Assessment Items

Standard: Understand the measurable attributes of objects and the units, systems, and process of measurement

Expectations

- Recognize the attribute of volume
- Understand how to measure using both nonstandard and standard units
- Communicate reasoning

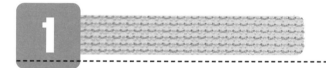

Will This Fit?

Grade range: Pre-K–1

About the mathematics: The "Will This Fit?" task yields insight into students' understanding of nonstandard measurement as it relates to volume. Students are asked to informally compare the volume of objects by predicting which items will successfully fit inside a box. Predicting focuses students' attention on the attribute being measured. In this task, the attribute being considered is the space occupied by an object. The task also serves as an assessment of students' developing spatial sense.

TASK

Show students an empty shoebox.

"Look at this shoebox. What is something from our classroom that will fit inside so that I can put the lid on without anything sticking out? What makes you think it will fit?"

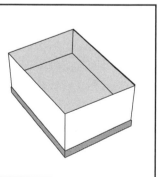

Using this assessment task: This task can be used with individuals, small groups, or large groups. Each student will need a blank sheet of paper. Show students a real shoebox, and leave it displayed where they can see it. As appropriate, ask students to draw or write about their ideas. You may choose to have students dictate their justifications and to record individual responses directly on the student's paper.

A common initial response from students is a shoe or a pair of shoes, so teachers may want to prompt students to think of items other than shoes. Placing the lid on the box can also be a real eye-opener for students, encouraging them to revise some of their predictions.

Solution: Because students select the objects they name, responses will vary. Each object chosen must be able to fit inside the shoebox with the lid closed. Examples of likely solutions are objects commonly found in classrooms, for example, a pencil, glue bottle, crayon, eraser, block, or connecting cubes.

Continuum of Understanding

Not Yet Started

- Gives no response, or responds with an object that is clearly too large to fit in the box

Developing Understanding

- Indicates an object that comes in a range of sizes, from those that could possibly fit to those that may not
- Interprets the task as being asked to fill the box with many of the same item, for example, may answer, "A hundred connecting cubes"
- Tries to find something that will fit "exactly," for example, may say, "The desk is way too big, the pencil is too small, but what will go right in?"

Strong Understanding

- Describes or represents an item, for example, a specific block, that will fit in the box so that the lid will close; may realize that more than one of those items could fit in the box at the same time but realizes that the question does not ask for that information
- Describes the position of the object, for example, "To make it fit, lay it on its side."
- Realizes that a given object, such as a piece of paper, may need to be folded or bent to make it fit in the box

Looking for Evidence of Understanding

Teachers in the pilot test noted that many students opted to draw a picture of a box containing their selected objects even though they were not asked to draw a box.

LaTonya: Not Yet Started

LaTonya drew a picture of a girl lying inside a box. When LaTonya's teacher asked her to describe the kind of girl she was thinking about, she responded by saying, "A girl like me."

Eddie: Developing Understanding

Eddie drew several pictures of a rectangular box containing various objects, including a book, plant, clock, eraser, basket, pencil, ruler, play dough, and scissors. Eddie asked his teacher

whether he could get those items and place them inside the box. After collecting and trying to place the items inside the box one at a time, Eddie was surprised to discover that some of the items did not fit once he attempted to place the lid on the box.

Laura: Strong Understanding

Laura chose to draw a variety of small objects that would fit inside the box, including a watch, a worm, and a spider, as well as some larger items that needed to be rolled or folded. Note that she realized that a piece of paper needed to be rolled and that a T-shirt could fit in the box if it was folded. Laura confidently told her teacher, "I bet if I roll a piece of paper, it will fit inside the box" and "If I folded my T-shirt, it could also fit inside the box."

Variations for the Range of Learners

This type of question may be too open-ended for some students. The teacher might choose to reframe the question to limit possible responses, for example, "Collect a variety of objects that will fit in the box with the lid on, and several that will not." Ask students to predict whether a specific item will fit and to explain why or why not without trying it out. Students who need more challenge could be asked to estimate how many of the same object could fit inside the box.

Standard: Understand the measurable attributes of objects and the units, systems, and processes of measurement

Expectations
- Recognize the attribute of time
- Compare and order objects according to [that attribute]
- Communicate reasoning

2

Before and After

Grade range: Pre-K–1

About the mathematics: Students build a strong foundation for their emerging understanding of measurement through exploring everyday situations. In this task, students are asked to sequence events as they identify and explain what comes before or after a given daily event. The "Before and After" task lends insight into students' initial understanding of time as an attribute of events and into their ability to order events on the basis of the attribute of time.

TASK

A. Tell me what might happen before you leave school. How did you decide? Tell me what might happen after you leave school. How did you decide?

B. Tell me what might happen before lunch. How did you decide? Tell me what might happen after lunch. How did you decide?

C. Tell me might happen before recess. How did you decide? Tell me what might happen after recess. How did you decide?

Using this assessment task: This task can be used with individuals, pairs, small groups, or large groups. Each student will need a copy of the three "Before and After" blackline masters. Teachers will need copies of the "Before and After Observation Form" blackline master. Younger students may be helped by being asked to first illustrate their responses and then to explain their illustrations orally. Teachers have also found that beginning writers often forget or skip the explanation portion of this task and may need assistance in writing their responses.

Solution: Possible solutions could include some of the following:

	Before		After	
Prompt	Event	Explanation	Event	Explanation
A	I go to centers and learn new things.	We go to centers while we are at school.	I watch television.	I always watch cartoons when I get home from school.
B	We go to the restroom to wash our hands.	We always wash our hands before we go to lunch.	We take a nap.	My teacher makes us take a nap after lunch.
C	We have computer class.	When we leave computer class, we go outside for recess.	We go to the water fountain.	Every day we get a drink after recess.

Continuum of Understanding

Indicators	Low Level	Medium Level	High Level
Does the student demonstrate an understanding of the problem?	No	Somewhat	Yes
Is the student able to identify what comes before and after each event?	No	Somewhat	Yes
Is the student able to justify his or her answers?	No	Somewhat	Yes

Looking for Evidence of Understanding

Myles: Low Level

Myles has a low understanding of what comes before and after lunch. He drew a picture of himself playing with a dog before lunch and reciting the Pledge of Allegiance with an announcement on the loud speaker after lunch. His teacher asked him whether he plays with his dog at home before he eats lunch, and he replied that he didn't have a dog. The Pledge of Allegiance is recited during morning announcements, not after lunch.

Anna: Medium Level

Before | After

1.) We mit board trnl math.
2.) We mit Play aVlanche.
We mit ned.
We eat luch
I waK home.
I watchTV.
I Play wit toys
I cach butterflys
cafe

Anna clearly drew and labeled pictures of events that occur before she leaves school and after she leaves school. However, when prompted, she was unable to justify her illustrations and sentences.

Madison: High Level

Before | After

We go to lunchs do langyege, spelling, and line up.
Becaus I da that evrey day. It is what I do.

We go in and get a drink and get ouer back Packs.
Becas We al was do that is why. Eryddy it is the same.

Madison clearly listed appropriate events that occur before and after recess. She also presented a written justification and was able verbally to expand on that justification when prompted by the teacher.

Variations for the Range of Learners

- Cut pictures from magazines, or draw pictures on cards and ask students to explain what might have happened before or after the event shown in the picture.
- Present students with a set of two to five cards showing routine events from the daily class schedule, and ask them to put the cards in the order in which the events occur.
- Ask students to sequence three events. Ask them to describe what happened yesterday, what happened today, and what might happen tomorrow.
- State a specific time, such as 9:00 a.m. Ask students to name something that happens before 9:00 a.m. and something that happens after 9:00 a.m.

Standards

- Understand measurable attributes of objects and the units, systems, and processes of measurement
- Apply appropriate techniques, tools, and formulas to determine measurements

Expectations

- Recognize and compare objects according to the attribute of area
- Develop a common referent for area to make comparisons and estimates
- Communicate mathematical reasoning

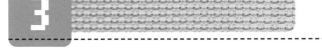

What Might Your Hand Cover?

Grade range: Pre-K–1

About the mathematics: Estimation activities focus students' attention on the attributes being measured. In the "What Might Your Hand Cover?" task, students employ strategies for estimating and comparing the area of objects using the size of their hand as a common referent. Specifically, students are asked to predict items that their hand will cover so that one cannot see what is underneath and to explain their reasoning.

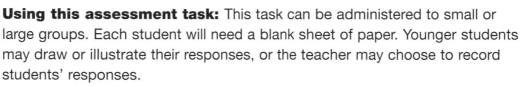

TASK

Look at your hand. What might you cover with your hand so that you could not see what was underneath? What makes you think your hand will cover it?

Using this assessment task: This task can be administered to small or large groups. Each student will need a blank sheet of paper. Younger students may draw or illustrate their responses, or the teacher may choose to record students' responses.

Be very specific in explaining to students that their hand must completely cover the object so that the object cannot be seen by others. Students often select small objects that their hand only partially covers, because they do not realize that their hand needs to cover the object completely. Teachers might want students to first trace their own hand to get a better sense of what objects their hand can actually cover.

Solution: The responses to this task will vary. Possible responses include such objects as an eraser, broken crayon, pattern block, dice, coins, bug, bead, and ring. Some students may select body parts, such as an eye, nose, ear, mole, birthmark, and lips, which are also acceptable responses. Another factor to keep in mind is that people's hands vary in size, so the size of the student's hand will also affect her or his responses.

Continuum of Understanding

Not There Yet

- Does not generate a solution or a response
- Responds with an object so large that it cannot possibly be covered with his or her hand

On Target

- Identifies an object that can typically be covered with a young child's hand
- Selects a small object that can clearly be covered completely with his or her hand, and gives a reasonable explanation for the choice

Going Beyond

- Identifies multiple items that can be covered completely, and gives an appropriate explanation
- Realizes that folding, bending, or scrunching a given item is needed so that it can be covered with her or his hand

Looking for Evidence of Understanding

Bethany: Not There Yet

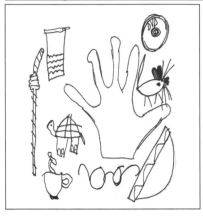

Bethany drew several objects, but unfortunately all the objects were too big and most could not possibly be covered with her hand. Bethany gave no response when her teacher asked her to explain her reasoning.

Diego: On Target

Diego drew a picture of an ant. His illustration and written response clearly indicate his ability to identify an object smaller than his hand.

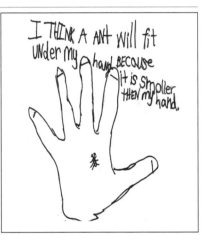

Cash: Going Beyond

Note that Cash's illustration indicates his awareness of ways an object can be changed to make it possible for his hand to completely cover it. Cash realized that by folding and crumpling a piece of paper, his hand was capable of covering the object completely.

Variations for the Range of Learners

- Display a variety of objects, and ask the student to identify or predict which objects can be covered completely with his or her hand.
- Allow students to test their predictions.
- Show a standard measuring reference, such as a piece of paper, to all the students. "Look around our room. What could you cover with a piece of paper so that you could not see what was underneath?"

Standard: Understand measurable attributes of objects and the units, systems, and processes of measurement

Expectations
- Recognize the attribute of length
- Compare and order objects according to length
- Use reasoning to make estimates and conjectures about measurement

---

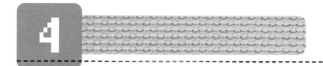

Longer or Shorter

Grade range: Pre-K–1

About the mathematics: The "Longer or Shorter" task assesses two aspects of students' understanding of linear measurement—length as an attribute and the ordering of objects by length. By estimating and then using direct comparison, students are to determine several objects that are longer than, shorter than, and the same length as a piece of string. Once five objects have been selected, students are required to do further comparisons among the objects to order them from shortest to longest.

TASK

1. Measure the distance around one of your knees with a piece of string. Cut the string to that length.
2. Using your piece of string to compare, find–
   - two objects that are longer than the piece of string;
   - two objects that are shorter than the piece of string; and
   - one object that is about the same length as the piece of string.

   Here are five small square pieces of paper. On each small square of paper, draw a picture of one of the objects you found or write down the name of one of the five objects you found.
3. Using the squares of paper that show the objects you found, order the objects from shortest to longest and then paste them on a sheet of paper.

Using this assessment task: This task is designed for use with the whole class; however, because some students may need assistance cutting their pieces of string, the teacher may choose to cut strings in advance. In addition to a piece of string, each student needs five small square pieces of paper. Squares that are approximately 4 inches by 4 inches work well.

Tell students to use a variety of objects for making comparisons. They can use objects they find at their table, such as pencils or scissors, or you can have them move about the classroom to measure posters, bins, plants, or books. As the students are locating the five objects, encourage them first to estimate or predict whether the object will be longer or shorter than their string and then to measure the object's length with the string. As the students are predicting and measuring, ask individual students, "Why do you think it will be shorter than (longer than, about the same length as) your string?"

Once students have selected and recorded the objects on the slips of paper, ask them to put the pieces of paper in order of length of the pictured object, from the shortest to the longest. For those students who drew pictures only, the teacher may find that writing the names of the pictured objects on the squares of paper for later reference is helpful.

Solution: The solutions will vary from student to student. A complete solution will include evidence that a student can focus on the attribute of length and can identify objects that are shorter than, longer than, and about the same length as a given piece of string. Make note of those students who confuse linear measurement with area or volume measurement and thus use such words as *smaller* and *bigger* rather than *shorter* and *longer*. The following shows one possible solution:

Shorter than string   Same length   Longer than string

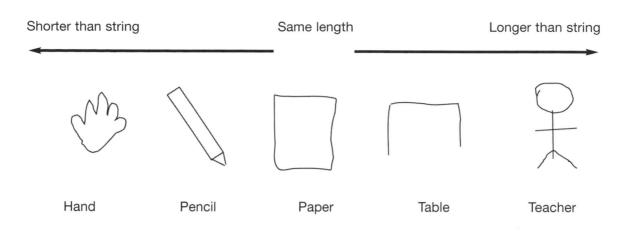

Hand   Pencil   Paper   Table   Teacher

Continuum of Understanding

	Not There Yet	Developing	On Target
Longer, shorter, and the same length	Has difficulty discerning objects that are longer, shorter, and the same length	Is able to visualize objects that are longer or shorter but may have difficulty determining objects that are close to the same length as the string; correctly measures to determine longer, shorter, or same length	Accurately determines through visualization items that are longer or shorter; correctly measures and confirms items that are longer, shorter, and the same length
Ordering objects	Is not able to order objects from shortest to longest	Requires some assistance in ordering objects from shortest to longest	Accurately and confidently orders objects from shortest to longest

Looking for Evidence of Understanding

Justin: Not There Yet

Justin did not attempt to use the string to measure objects but eventually drew a picture to represent a table. He responded with shoulder shrugs and "I don't know" to prompts to find another object longer than the string. When asked to find objects shorter than the string, Justin drew a picture of a chair. Justin left the pictures as they were when the teacher asked him to put the pictures in order of length.

Asha: Measuring—Developing; Ordering—Not There Yet

Asha walked around the room and used the string to measure different objects until she found one that seemed to fit the specified category. She identified the chart stand as a longer object and a crayon as a shorter object. However, she was not able to order the items according to length, and her descriptions of the order indicated some confusion about ordering. Asha also mixed linear measurement terms (i.e., *longest, shortest*) with other terminology related to size (i.e., *medium, a little smaller,* and *smallest*).

Davina: Developing

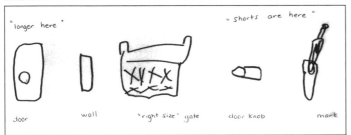

Davina first estimated the lengths of objects and then used the string to verify their lengths by measuring. Once she measured some objects, she eliminated them if she discovered that her estimate was not accurate according to the specified category (longer, shorter, or the same length). She measured several objects that she estimated would be about the same length as the string and persisted until she found an object (a stairway gate) that was almost exactly the same length as the string. When asked to order the objects according to length, Davina sorted them into three categories: longer, shorter, and the "right size." She did not place them in order of length within the categories.

Kai: On Target

Kai readily identified objects that he estimated to be longer than, shorter than, and the same length as the string. He used the string to verify that the size of the chair seat was about the same length as the string but relied on visualization to confirm his choices of items longer than and shorter than the string. Kai labeled two objects as shorter than the string and two objects as longer than the string. He ordered the objects within those categories and numbered the pictures of the objects from 1 to 5 (shortest to longest).

Variations for the Range of Learners

- For students with less experience, the teacher can limit the items from which they may choose by selecting several objects that are much more linear in shape (e.g., straws, pencils, paper tubes, sentence strips, chalk tray.
- Challenge more-experienced students by stipulating that the objects chosen cannot be more than a hand width longer or shorter than the string.

Standard: Understand the measurable attributes of objects and the units, systems, and processes of measurement

Expectations
- Recognize the attribute of weight
- Compare objects according to weight
- Reason using visualizations
- Communicate mathematical thinking

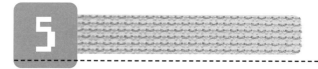

Is This Possible?

Grade range: Pre-K–1

About the mathematics: One of the ways we measure things is by weighing them. Students should have numerous opportunities for explorations involving weight because such experiences can provide them with valuable information about their surroundings. Weighing an assortment of objects also offers students a real-life application of measurement. In the "Is This Possible?" task, students are asked to compare two pictures of animals on a seesaw and convey whether the situation pictured is possible or impossible. This task assesses students' understanding of weight as an attribute and of comparing objects to conclude which is lighter or heavier.

TASK

Look at picture 1. Is this situation possible or impossible? Tell me why you think it is possible or not possible.

Picture 1

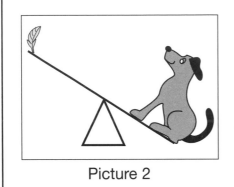

Picture 2

Look at picture 2. Is this situation possible? Tell me why you think it is possible or not possible.

Using this assessment task: This task is designed to be used with individual students or small groups. Each student will need a copy of the "Is This Possible?" blackline master. Teachers of younger students might need to discuss the meaning of *possible* and *impossible* prior to presenting the task. Explain to students that the pictures of the animals on the seesaw represent real animals, not stuffed animals or toys. Teachers of younger students may prefer to record students' justifications.

Solution: The following are examples of appropriate solutions:

The situation in picture 1 is impossible because a bear is without a doubt heavier than a mouse. The seesaw should be tilting the opposite way to make the situation possible.

Picture 2 is possible because a feather is definitely lighter than the dog. The seesaw is correctly balanced.

Continuum of Understanding

Limited Evidence

Shows little or no understanding of comparative weights and is unable to explain his or her response

Adequate Evidence

Shows that she or he understands the concept of comparing weights but is unable to clearly communicate her or his reasoning

Strong Evidence

Shows that he or she clearly understands comparative weights and is able to clearly communicate appropriate reasoning

Looking for Evidence of Understanding

Anton: Limited Evidence

Anton circled the word *possible* for picture 1 and circled *impossible* for picture 2. Both of Anton's responses were incorrectly answered, and when prompted, he was not able to furnish any reasoning for his responses.

Lauren: Adequate Evidence

Lauren correctly answered both questions, but her reasoning was insufficient. For picture 1, Lauren stated, "Because it can't." For picture 2, she stated, "Because it can."

Ricardo: Strong Evidence

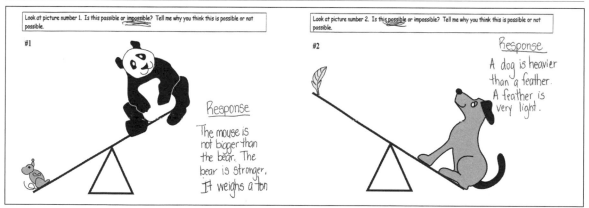

Ricardo underlined the correct answers for both pictures. He explained to his teacher, "The mouse is not bigger than the bear. The bear is stronger. It weighs a ton." For picture number 2, he stated, "A dog is heavier than a feather. A feather is very light."

Variations for the Range of Learners

- Place twenty items of the same thing into resealable plastic bags—for example, twenty cotton balls, twenty pennies, twenty feathers, twenty rocks, or twenty paper clips. Have students predict and explain which collection of objects is heaviest or lightest.
- Ask students to draw pictures of things that are light and of things that are heavy.
- Have students cut pictures from magazines, or provide them with a set of pictures and ask them to create a picture of a seesaw arrangement that is possible and one that is impossible.
- Remove the stipulation that the objects presented in the task must be "real" animals or a "real" feather. What would have to be true about the objects to make each situation possible? What would have to be true about the objects to make each situation impossible?

Standards
- Understand the measurable attributes of objects and the units, systems, and processes of measurement
- Apply appropriate techniques, tools, and formulas to determine measurements

Expectations
- Recognize the attribute of length
- Understand how to measure using nonstandard units
- Measure with multiple copies of units of the same size
- Make reasonable estimates using visualization

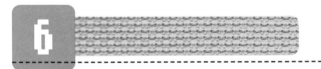

Six Straws

Grade range: Pre-K–2

About the mathematics: In measuring with standard units, we might ask, "What is the length of the table?" Another measuring question is "How long is 25 centimeters?" The "Six Straws" task uses nonstandard units to focus on the latter question. In this task students make a linear estimate of a specified number of nonstandard units (e.g., 6) for two different-sized units, such as coffee stir sticks and straws. The task helps teachers assess students' ability to (1) measure using nonstandard units by placing the units in a line without gaps or overlaps; (2) make a reasonable estimate of a specified number of units; and (3) make a new estimate of the same quantity using a different unit.

TASK

Estimate Stir Sticks: I have six stir sticks. If you lined them up, how far would they stretch from beginning to end? Take one block to mark where you will start (block 1), and put the other block where you think six stir sticks will end (block 2). How did you decide how far apart to put the blocks?

Try it: How long is the line of six stir sticks? Tell me as you put each stir stick down whether you think your estimate is too short, too long, or okay. (Allow the student to arrange the six stir sticks in a line and to reflect on his or her estimate.) Next take your other block (block 2), and put it at the end of the six lined-up stir sticks.

Estimate Straws: Here are six straws. If you lined them up, how far would they stretch? Will the line be longer or shorter than the line of six stir sticks? Starting at the same place as for the stir sticks (block 1), make a new estimate and place another block (block 3) where you think six straws will end.

Try it: How long is the line of six straws? Tell me as you put them down whether you think your estimate is too short, too long, or okay.

Using this assessment task: This task is designed to be done in small groups of two to four students. Each student will need to have two sets of six units of different lengths (e.g., toothpicks, stir sticks, straws, unsharpened pencils, paper clips, craft sticks). They will also need three markers for the beginning and end of their estimates (e.g., blocks, sticky notes). The teacher can make copies of the "Six Straws: Checklist" blackline master for documenting students' responses.

As students make their estimates, ask them to explain the basis for their reasoning. Some students may imagine putting the six units down end to end; some may think about the length of three units and then make their estimate twice as long; others may make physical estimates using their hands as substitute units.

Solution: The estimation and actual measurement will depend on the objects chosen. Listen for the following estimation strategies and explanations:

- "I imagined how far three would be and then three more."
- "I pretended to put them down and put the block down when I got to six."
- Student uses a hand or a foot as a substitute, and measures.

For the second unit estimate:

- "I know it will be farther because the straws are longer than the stir sticks."
- "The straws are longer by this much [shows distance with fingers]. So I need to put the block six of these farther."

Continuum of Understanding

First Unit Criteria	Y = Yes; S = Somewhat; N = No
Makes a reasonable estimate for the first unit	
Communicates a useful estimation method	
Applies appropriate measuring technique by lining up units without gaps or overlaps	
Is able to determine whether estimate is too long or too short in the process of measuring	

Second Unit Criteria	Y = Yes; S = Somewhat; N = No
Makes a reasonable estimate for the second unit by using the information gained from the first measuring task	
Communicates that the distance is longer/shorter because the units are longer/shorter	
Applies appropriate measuring technique	
Is able to determine whether estimate is too long or too short in the process of measuring	

Looking for Evidence of Understanding

Holly: Limited Understanding

This task was presented with pencils and toothpicks to Holly. Her initial estimate for the length of six pencils was very short. She tried to match the pencils to her estimate by overlapping the pencils as shown in the photograph. In using toothpicks as the second unit, Holly used the same estimate as in the first task. This time she did not overlap the toothpicks as she measured the distance. She knew that the toothpicks were shorter than the pencils, but she was not able to relate that relationship to estimating the length of six of them.

Name: Holly

First Unit: Pencils	Y = Yes; S = Somewhat; N = No
Makes a reasonable estimate for the first unit	No
Communicates a useful estimation method	No
Applies appropriate measuring technique by lining up units without gaps or overlaps	No
Is able to determine whether estimate is too long or too short in the process of measuring	No

Second Unit: Toothpicks	Y = Yes; S = Somewhat; N = No
Makes a reasonable estimate for the second unit by using the information gained from the first measuring task	No
Communicates that the distance is longer/shorter because the units are longer/shorter	Somewhat
Applies appropriate measuring technique	Somewhat
Is able to determine whether estimate is too long or too short in the process of measuring	No

Alex: Strong Understanding

Alex predicted the length of the stir sticks by using his hand as a referent. As he began putting down the stir sticks, he said, "My hands were uneven" and adjusted his estimate. He compared the straw with the stir stick and noticed that it was about two times longer, so he made his estimate of the lined-up straws twice as long.

Name: Alex

First Unit: Stir Sticks	Y = Yes; S = Somewhat; N = No
Makes a reasonable estimate for the first unit	Somewhat
Communicates a useful estimation method	Yes
Applies appropriate measuring technique by lining up units without gaps or overlaps	Yes
Is able to determine whether estimate is too long or too short in the process of measuring	Yes

Second Unit: Straws	Y = Yes; S = Somewhat; N = No
Makes a reasonable estimate for the second unit by using the information gained from the first measuring task	Yes
Communicates that the distance is longer/shorter because the units are longer/shorter	Yes
Applies appropriate measuring technique	Yes
Is able to determine whether estimate is too long or too short in the process of measuring	Yes

Variations for the Range of Learners

The task as written uses a limited number of units to allow younger students to participate without being challenged by the need to count large numbers. To make the task more challenging, the teacher may use ten or more units. To assess the process of measuring in more depth, suppy only one unit (e.g., one straw) and observe whether students are able to employ ten repetitions of the single unit. For example, they may use a finger to mark the end of the straw, then pick up the straw and put it down without a significant gap or overlap.

When students with less experience are visualizing distances, they may require additional support. For example, the teacher may lay out six sticks end to end on the table. The student is then required to use two blocks to estimate the length of six lined-up sticks on the floor (or at a location that is somewhat removed from the six sticks). The student then places the six sticks end to end starting at one of the blocks to check her or his estimate.

Standard: Understand the measurable attributes of objects and the units, systems, and processes of measurement

Expectation:

- Recognize the attribute of weight
- Estimate, compare, and order objects according to weight
- Understand how to measure using nonstandard units
- Make and investigate mathematical conjectures
- Communicate mathematical reasoning

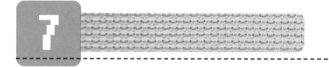

Ordering Objects by Weight

Grade range: Pre-K–2

About the mathematics: The "Ordering Objects by Weight" task assesses students' proficiency at the process of measuring more than two objects. Students are asked to order three objects by weight—first by observation, then by feel, and finally by the use of a pan balance. The task requires students to develop a systematic method for comparing the three objects.

TASK

Look: Here are three objects (e.g., toy car, box of crayons, stuffed animal). Without touching the objects, which one do you think is heaviest? Lightest? In between? Why do you think so?

Touch: Compare the objects by holding them in your hands. Now which do you think is heaviest? Lightest? In between? Did your order change?

Measure: Using a pan balance, compare the objects. Which is heaviest? Lightest? In between? Did your order change?

Using this assessment task: The materials needed for this task include a pan balance and at least three objects that vary in weight and size. Include some items that are small but heavy and some that are large but light; the assortment might include such objects as a stuffed animal, book, bean bag, wooden block, and piggy bank. The task can be set up as a station, at which one to two students can be assessed at one time. At each of the three stages in the task—Look, Touch, Measure—encourage students to record the predicted or measured order of the objects. Furnishing a structured worksheet may assist some students.

The teacher should keep anecdotal records and note the student's progress in three aspects of performance being assessed: his or her (1) subjective expectations, (2) ability to order three objects, and (3) measuring process.

Subjective expectations. Less-experienced students typically assume that the larger objects are heavier. Listen to determine whether students refer to objects as "smaller" and "bigger" rather than "lighter" and "heavier." That misconception is more likely if the objects are unfamiliar to the student. An essential aspect of the assessment, however, is not whether students' initial guess is correct but whether they are willing to alter their ordering when confronted with evidence gathered in the touching and measuring phases.

Ordering three objects. Although the words *heaviest* and *lightest* are learned early on, less-experienced students may have difficulty when three objects are involved and may describe one as "heavier" and the other two as "lighter." The prompt suggests using the terms *lightest, heaviest,* and *in between.* However, to encourage students to find the middle object, the teacher may suggest that they order the items from heaviest to lightest or determine which object is neither the heaviest nor the lightest.

Measuring process. Look at the students' process of comparing the three objects. Do they use a reliable strategy that will lead to proper ordering? For example, one systematic approach would be to choose the heaviest object and confirm that it is heaviest by comparing it with the other two objects individually. Next, the student could compare the remaining two objects to determine which is heavier or lighter. The use of the pan balance may be challenging for some students. Determine whether the difficulty stems from their lack of familiarity with the pan balance or whether they do not know a means of comparing the three objects.

Solution: The final solution will vary depending on the objects selected. A complete solution will include evidence that a student can successfully use a pan balance to compare and order three objects from lightest to heaviest.

Continuum of Understanding

	Initial Understanding	Developing Understanding	Strong Understanding
Expectations	Uses "smaller" and "bigger" to describe objects; orders objects by size	Uses a combination of size and weight to make ordering decisions	Refers to the expected weight of the materials to determine the order
Ordering three objects	May identify lightest and heaviest but does not identify a "middle" object; places it with heaviest or lightest object	Requires prompting to determine a "middle" object	Has no difficulty ordering three objects
Measuring process	Uses feel and perhaps the pan balance to determine the heaviest object but does not know a means of comparing all three	Uses feel and perhaps the pan balance to determine a heavy and a light object but may neglect comparisons with the third object	Uses feel and a pan balance to systematically compare all three objects and place them in an appropriate order

Looking for Evidence of Understanding

Georgia: Initial and Developing Understanding

The three objects used were a scientific calculator, a tin of pennies, and an empty box. Georgia is at the level of "Developing Understanding" for expectations and ordering three objects. From her observation of the three objects, she stated, "The calculator is the lightest. The box is the biggest." Here she used a combination of weight and size terminology to make comparisons. Georgia did not identify a middle object on her own, although she said yes when the teacher prompted her by asking whether the tin was in the middle. When Georgia picked up the objects, she stated that the calculator and the box were "both about the same amount" and that the tin was "definitely the heaviest."

Georgia was at the level of "Initial Understanding" for the measuring process. She put the tin in one pan and the other two objects in the other pan of the pan balance and easily identified the tin as the heaviest. She did not have a strategy, to identify the order of the other two objects. She did not realize she could identify the order of the other two objects by measuring them, or by weighing them. Her lack of experience with the pan balance caused her difficulty in using that tool.

Jessica: Strong Understanding

The three objects used were a calculator, a large empty box, and a wooden apple. The teacher used a chart like the following to record Jessica's responses and to make comments. Although the box was the largest object, Jessica did not assume it was the heaviest. She compared the three objects systematically and had no difficulty ordering them from lightest to heaviest.

Prompt	Lightest	Middle	Heaviest	Explanation/Comments
Look	Apple	Box	Calculator	Looks at objects and guesses
Touch	Box	Apple	Calculator	"Now I'm going to see for sure." Picks up the box, "Ahhh, this is the lightest!" Picks up the calculator, "That's what I thought. This is the heaviest, and this [the apple] is in the middle."
Measure	Box	Apple	Calculator	Compares the calculator (heaviest) with the apple. Compares the box (lightest) with the apple. Compares the box (lightest) with the calculator (heaviest). Explains that she knows she is right by noticing when the balance tips down. "So I'm right! The box never touched the bottom, so this is the lightest. And the apple touched once, so the apple is in the middle."

Variations for the Range of Learners

- For students who lack experience in making heavier-lighter comparisons, the task can be restricted to comparing two items.
- The difficulty of the task can be increased by using more than three objects. The process of comparing four or five objects must be approached systematically by the student.
- The task can be made more challenging by using collections of objects rather than single objects. For example, students could compare collections of five marbles, ten pencils, and seven erasers.

Standard: Understand the measurable attributes of objects and the units, systems, and processes of measurement

Expectations
- Recognize the attribute of time
- Communicate mathematical thinking
- Make connections among mathematical ideas

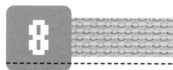

More Time—Less Time

Grade range: K–1

About the mathematics: Comparing two or more objects or events strengthens students' development and understanding of measurement attributes. In the "More Time—Less Time" task, students compare and order four or more destinations with respect to duration of time. Time can be thought of as the duration of an event from its beginning to its end. This task assesses students' understanding of time as the duration of the trip to each of four travel destinations. They must consider which trip would require more travel time and which would require less travel time.

TASK

Cut apart the six cards on the "More Time–Less Time" blackline master.

A. Show the four cards with the pictures. "These cards show four destinations, or places where you might go—the stars, the school restroom, the school playground, and your home. Which destination would take you the longest time to reach from our classroom? Put the four cards in order, from the destination taking the least travel time to the one taking the most travel time. Then tell me why you placed them in that order."

B. "On the blank cards, draw two other destinations of your choice. Next, order all six cards from least travel time to most travel time. Then glue the cards on the paper in order. Finally, tell me why you placed them in that order."

Using this assessment task: This task is designed to be administered to small groups or individuals. Each student needs a copy of the blackline master "More Time–Less Time"; a pair of scissors; a long strip of paper (e.g., sentence strip); glue; and drawing tools, such as pencils and crayons. Teachers may choose to use the "More Time–Less Time Observation Form" to record students' responses and explanations.

Teachers need to explain each of the four pictures to students before asking them to cut the cards apart. Including a label for each picture may be helpful, especially for younger students. Some teachers suggest creating two additional cards, labeled "least" and "most," for students to glue at each end of their paper strip, explaining that *least* means the shortest amount of travel time and that *most* means the longest amount of travel time.

Solution: The answers will vary depending on the location of the four destinations from the classroom. The most likely arrangement of the four cards is (1) school restroom, (2) school playground, (3) home, and (4) stars. Students should be able to explain that certain destinations are closer than others and therefore require less travel time; for example, the school restroom may be the closest, whereas the stars are the farthest, so they require the most travel time.

The order of the six cards will vary depending on what two additional destinations each student chooses to illustrate. Examples of destinations that students have illustrated include the cafeteria, library, office, gym, nurse's office, park, store, mall, lake, museum, movie theatre, beach, mountains, forest, and vacation spots. Students' justifications for the order of their cards should furnish evidence of their understanding of which destinations would require more travel time and which would require less travel time.

Continuum of Understanding

Observation Form			
Understands Problem	Level of Understanding	Explanations	Anecdotal Comments
Complete understanding			
Partial understanding			
Misunderstanding			
Solves Problem			
Orders all destinations correctly			
Orders some of the destinations correctly			
Is unsuccessful at ordering the destinations			
Communicates Reasoning			
Gives clear, concise, and correct explanation			
Give good but not completely clear explanation			
Gives insufficient explanation			

Looking for Evidence of Understanding

Teachers found the task easier to use by recording students' explanations, either because young students required a long time to write their responses or because their responses were short and vague. Students who were asked to explain their reasoning orally provided more detailed responses that fostered more insight into their understanding.

Hong: Low Level of Understanding

Hong was unsuccessful at ordering the destination cards from least to most time. Although he placed the restroom card first, he was unable to place the remaining cards in the correct order. Hong glued his cards in this order: (1) school restroom, (2) stars, (3) mountains, (4) his house, (5) city, and (6) school playground. Hong could not justify his card arrangement.

Joseph: Medium Level of Understanding

Joseph arranged the cards from the most to the least travel time rather than in the reverse order requested. His explanation confirmed that he had confused the meanings of *most* and *least*. He stated, "I glued the cards from least to most. First come the stars. The ocean comes next, then my house. Then it's the playground, the library, and the last place is the restroom."

Presley: High Level of Understanding

Presley quickly ordered the cards from the least to the most travel time. She confidently gave reasons for her arrangement: "I put the restroom first because it is the closest to me. It takes me a short time to walk to the restroom. I put the stars picture last because it is far, far away. It is the longest place because you have to ride a rocket to get there. It takes a long, long, long time to reach the stars. The cafeteria comes after the restroom because it is down the hall. The playground is across the street from our school, so it goes next. I think my house comes next because I have to get in our car to get there. The Florida beach is next because we fly a big airplane to get to the beach. Last is the stars card."

Variations for the Range of Learners

* Have students order more destinations or fewer destinations.
* Present students with three tasks, such as tying a shoe, taking a bath, or taking out the trash, and ask them to predict which task would require the most time to accomplish.
* Present students with three destinations within their school. Ask them to think about walking to each place and to predict which would require the most walking time: office, gym, or library. Students should explain their predictions.
* Ask students to estimate how many seconds, minutes, or hours the walk to each destination would take.

Standard: Apply appropriate techniques, tools, and formulas to determine measurements

Expectations

- Use the repetition of a single nonstandard unit to measure something larger than the unit itself
- Use tools to measure
- Use reasoning to estimate quantities
- Communicate mathematical thinking to others

How Many Blocks?

Grade range: K–2

About the mathematics: This task lends insight into students' understanding of the measurement process for weight and of the result of using different units for measuring the weight of objects. The measurement process involves choosing a unit, comparing that unit with the object, and reporting the number of units used. Students are asked to weigh an object using a nonstandard unit and then to predict the results of weighing the same object with a different nonstandard unit. The task allows the teacher to assess students' understanding of measurement as a form of balancing as well as their ability to estimate and compare two types of measuring units. Experiences that involve such comparison of units establish the foundation for students' eventual realization that different units give different levels of precision for their measurements.

TASK

Estimate how many blocks the pair of scissors weighs. Then use the pan balance to find out.

If you weighed the scissors with tiles, would you need more or fewer tiles than you needed blocks? Describe your thinking, and then find out.

Did you find a difference when using blocks compared with using tiles? Why do you think that difference occurred?

Using this assessment task: This task can be set up as a station at which the teacher assesses one or two students at a time. The materials needed include a pan balance, an object to weigh (e.g., toy, book, mug, scissors, key), and two types of nonstandard units that vary in size, shape, and weight (e.g., dominoes, plastic cubes, pencils, pennies, bottle caps, or blocks). Test the items to ensure that the number of units required to balance the object is within the counting capabilities of the students. For young learners, the number of units needed to balance an object should be fewer than ten. Older students can be given heavier objects and a larger variety of heavy and light units. The teacher should make anecdotal records of the students' estimations, results, and explanations.

Solution: The solutions to this task will vary depending on the specific objects and units used. A complete solution includes evidence that a student can focus on the attribute of weight, make a reasonable estimate, and use a pan balance to find a balance between the units and the object. Additionally, the student must demonstrate an understanding of the relationship between the two types of units—realizing that different units often result in different measurements and that using a lighter unit requires more of that unit to balance an object than does using a heavier unit.

Continuum of Understanding

Questions	Low Level	Moderate Level	High Level
Is the student's estimate reasonable?	No	Somewhat	Yes
Is the student able to balance the object with nonstandard units?	Is unable to find a balance	Yes, but requires some assistance	Yes, has no difficulty
Is the student able to determine whether the estimate was too high or too low?	Does not connect the estimate and the measurement	Yes, but may be hesitant	Yes; may also state the difference
Is the student able to estimate whether balancing the object with the second nonstandard unit will require more or fewer units?	No, is unable to state whether more or fewer are needed	Yes, but may be hesitant	Yes; may also estimate how many more or fewer are needed
Is the student able to explain why the results are different, that is, why one type of unit may require more than the other type?	No, does not connect the weight of units with the number of units required	Gives partial or incomplete explanation	Yes, refers to weight of both units; knows that fewer heavier units are required than lighter units

Looking for Evidence of Understanding

Many students realized that the different results related to differences in the weight of the two unit items. However, some students were not able to reconcile the inverse nature of the relationship, that is, needing more of the lighter units and fewer of the heavier units to balance the object.

Dylan: Low Level

Dylan said that he did not know how many cubes would be needed to balance a pen. With prompting, he indicated that probably "lots of them" or "a handful" would be needed. When he began to measure, he added cubes by handfuls to both sides of the balance. He commented that the scale "doesn't make any sense" and then pushed down on the lighter side with his hand so that the sides appeared to be balanced. Dylan estimated that the same number of tiles as cubes would be required to balance the pen and, as before, added tiles to both sides of the scale to measure.

Mackenzie: Moderate Level

Mackenzie predicted that she would need four cubes to balance the key and placed four cubes in the pan. The two pans were not quite balanced, so she said, "Maybe we should put more in" and added cubes until the balance shifted. She commented, "Now this is too heavy ... take some out." She removed cubes until the pans balanced (with six cubes), and declared, "That looks good." Using tiles as the second unit,

Mackenzie predicted that six tiles would probably be needed to balance the key, initially assuming that the cubes and tiles weighed the same amount. She placed six tiles in the pan, observed that the object was not balanced, and said, "Guess these [tiles] are lighter." She continued to add tiles until she achieved a balance with twelve tiles and observed that more tiles than cubes were needed "because they were lighter."

Alex: High Level

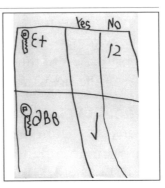

Alex predicted that three tiles would be needed to balance a key and then measured appropriately to determine the actual weight, which was 12 tiles. When asked to predict the weight using small unit cubes, he placed one cube on one side of the pan balance and one tile on the other. The tile was heavier than the cube. Alex said, "Tiles weigh more than blocks, and I think two cubes weigh one tile." He then added one cube to the scale to check. The scale was just slightly off balance, and Alex observed that two cubes were a "bit too heavy." He used the information to predict the weight of the key to be 23 because it was just less than double the actual weight of the key in tiles. When he measured, the actual weight was 23 cubes. Alex used a table to record his results and considered the measured results according to whether they did (yes) or did not (no) match the estimates.

Variations for the Range of Learners

To lessen the difficulty of the task, choose units that clearly differ in weight, one being much heavier than the other. To increase the challenge of the task, have students use the pan balance to compare the units prior to making their second estimate. Then ask students to predict how many of the other unit are needed.

5

Data Analysis and Probability

WE ARE confronted daily with information from television, the Internet, newspapers, and other sources. From an early age, children need to develop critical thinking skills and be able to make decisions based on data. They need to be able to ask good questions, use data wisely, evaluate claims that are based on data, and formulate defensible conclusions in the face of uncertainty.

Data analysis and probability offer tremendous opportunities for children to develop their innate sense of curiosity. Students experience problems and situations that lend themselves to the application of ideas that connect with other strands of mathematics, with other school subjects, and with various aspects of daily life. Students have opportunities to discover and use tools that will enable them to gather information that will help them answer some of their questions.

The data analysis and probability assessment tasks in this chapter address important content areas in the strand, including formulating questions; collecting, organizing, and displaying data; analyzing data through appropriate methods; and developing and evaluating inferences and predictions on the basis of data.

Formulate Questions

In the early grades, children are primarily interested in themselves and their immediate surroundings. They need opportunities to formulate questions closely related to their experience, for example, tasks that offer assessment opportunities to answer such questions as How many? What kind? Which of these? I wonder? and What is your favorite?

Collect, Organize, and Display Data

A fundamental idea in prekindergarten through second grade (pre-K–2) is that data can be collected, organized, and displayed in a way that provides information about the phenomenon or question being explored. Informal comparing, classifying, and counting activities are used to develop young learners' understanding of data collection and organization and allow them to begin to analyze their data. Many of the tasks included in this chapter offer opportunities for young learners to demonstrate their understanding of data and their ability to collect, organize, and display data, including "Alphabet Letters Sort," "I Wonder," "What Is Your Favorite?" "Do You Have All the Information You Need?" "Picking Possibilities," and "Paper-Clip Spin." By second grade, students will have learned a variety of ways to represent data using concrete objects, pictures, and graphs, including counts, tallies, frequency tables, bar graphs, concrete graphs, line plots, picture graphs, and Venn diagrams.

Analyze Data

Students in grades pre-K–2 are beginning to learn to analyze data collected to answer their own questions and support their conclusions. They are also beginning to make predictions based on the data. Students' analysis of data is informal at this level. Their analysis includes determining whether a given quantity is more or less than another as well as how many of each thing are present; it may also begin to compare parts of the data and make statements about the data as a whole by noting patterns or results that are more or less frequent in comparison with others.

Basic Concepts and Applications of Probability

Young children are just beginning to develop concepts of probability and should have opportunities to recognize how probability and statistics are related. The task "Is It Likely?" assesses children's acquisition of appropriate vocabulary to describe chance events, for example, the use of such words as *probably, unlikely, possibly, maybe, impossible,* and *certain.* Informal concepts of probability are further developed by engaging in activities, games, and experiments with concrete objects. The tasks "Is It Fair?" "Picking Possibilities," and "Prediction Game" assess students' basic concepts of probability and allow them to formulate conjectures and make decisions on the basis of their experiences and through the data they have collected.

Standards
- Formulate questions that can be addressed with data and collect, organize, and display relevant data to answer them
- Select and use appropriate statistical methods to analyze the data

Expectations
- Sort and classify objects according to their attributes and organize data about the objects
- Represent data using concrete objects, pictures, and graphs
- Describe parts of the data and the set of data as a whole to determine what the data show
- Create and use representations to organize, record, and communicate mathematical ideas

1

Alphabet Letters Sort

Grade Range: Pre-K–2

About the mathematics: The "Alphabet Letters Sort" task asks students to sort the alphabet letters according to their own rules and then represent the data using a method of their choosing, such as a bar graph, Venn diagram, or other means to demonstrate their sorted categories. Once the display is created, students should be instructed to interpret the information displayed, either verbally or in writing. The manner in which the students interpret the information fosters insight into their understanding of number and numerical relationships.

TASK

1. Spread out the alphabet letter cards on a table.
2. Look at the letters, and think about the following: How are the letters alike? How are the letters different?
3. Think about how the letters could be sorted. Sort the letters according to your own rules.
4. Create a display to show how you sorted the letters. Glue your letters onto a large sheet of paper. Name the rules you used.
5. Write or say what your display tells you about the letters.

A	B	C	D
E	F	G	H
I	J	K	L
M	N	O	P
Q	R	S	T
U	V	W	X
Y	Z		

Using this assessment task: This task can be used with the whole class. In advance, make a copy of the "Alphabet Letters" blackline master for each student and cut out the letter cards. Place each set of letters in an envelope or plastic bag. Provide students with a set of letters, scissors, glue or tape, a pencil, and paper to make their display.

Prior to sorting the letters, encourage students to look at how the letters are alike and different. They may determine their own set of rules involving two or more categories. If students have difficulty determining categories to create, the teacher may prompt them to look at the types of lines that are used; for example, some letters have straight lines, some have curved lines, and some have both.

Watch for students to sort the letters using a consistent set of rules and to create a display that clearly represents the rules used. Some categories may overlap (e.g., curved, straight, both), so the student will need to devise a way to show the overlap using a form of Venn diagram.

Students should use their display to identify and record their observations. For example, students may use numbers to count the number of letters in each category. They may make such comparisons as "more than" or "less than." The teacher may need to prompt students to make and record the comparisons by asking, "Which category has the most letters? How many does it have?"

Solution: An appropriate solution is one in which a student sorts the letters into two or more categories according to a consistent set of rules. All the letters should be placed into a category. Many rules can be used to sort the letters. Students may focus on the types of lines—straight, curved, vertical, horizontal, or diagonal—or the number of lines needed—one line (e.g., C and S), two lines (e.g., T and Q), three lines (e.g., Y and A), and so on. Other students may focus on the meaning of the letters—for example, the letters in their first name, last name, both names, or neither name.

The displays will vary. Each display should appropriately represent the categories chosen and allow the reader to make sense of the rules used. Some students may produce a bar graph or a Venn diagram. However, any presentation that displays the sorted letters in some manner is sufficient as long as the sorted groups and labels are clear.

Finally, the student should be able to make three or more observations about the display.

The following display shows one possible solution:

Straight	A	E	F	H	I	K	L	M	N	T	V	W	X	Y	Z
Curved	C	O	S	U											
Both	B	D	G	P	Q	R	J								

Sample Student Observations

- There are 15 letters that have only straight lines. That is the most.
- Four letters have [only] curved lines. That is the least.
- Seven letters have both curved and straight lines.
- There are more letters that have only straight lines (15) than letters that have a curved line in [them] (11).

Continuum of Understanding

Limited Evidence of Understanding

- Uses sorting rules that are unclear, or does not attempt to sort the letters
- Creates a display that does not clearly distinguish discernible categories
- Makes observations that are not related to the displayed data

Adequate Evidence of Understanding

- Uses clear but inconsistent rules to sort letters, and misplaces some letters
- Adequately displays data, and makes some attempt to label the categories
- Makes one or two observations using displayed data
- Produces a response that may require some inferences by the teacher

Strong Evidence of Understanding

- Uses clear, consistent rules to sort the letters
- Clearly and accurately displays and details the data
- Makes three or more observations and comparisons about the displayed data using numbers, comparisons, and other descriptions
- Produces a response that requires little, if any, inferring by the teacher

Looking for Evidence of Understanding

Manipulative models of the alphabet letters were used with younger children because they found the manipulatives easier to sort than cut-out paper versions. Several of the children who demonstrated limited evidence of understanding did not sort the letters into categories but instead compared letters two at a time and described their similarities. For example, when comparing **E** and **F**, one student explained, "F just needs another line to make E." When comparing **A** and **M**, another student stated, "If this didn't have a line across and had another bump up, it would be M." Other children who did not sort the letters into categories counted, or attempted to count, the number of letters.

Katianne: Limited Evidence

Katianne simply selected letters that she was familiar with and was able to name. She began by selecting the letters in her name. When prompted to sort the letters into groups, she stated that all the letters were different and did not attempt to sort them.

Emma: Adequate Evidence

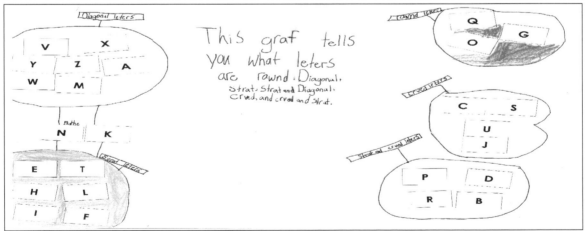

[This graph tells you what the letters are. Round. Diagonal. Straight. Straight and Diagonal. Curved, and curved and straight.]

This work shows letters sorted according to six different categories with one group containing the letters **N** and **K** placed between the group of "diagonal letters" and "straight letters" to indicate that they fit into "both" categories. Emma did not create a similar visual overlap for letters that have both straight lines and curved lines but instead created a separate group labeled "straight and curved letters" for that category. She displayed and clearly labeled the groups of letters. Emma explained that the graph shows different categories of letters and listed the categories. She did not offer discussions, observations, or comparisons specific to the data.

Jenna: Strong Evidence

Jenna used clear rules to sort the letters. She labeled the categories "all straight" and "all curve," and she organized the diagram to indicate an intersection of the two categories where letters with combinations of straight and curved lines are placed. She consistently sorted the data, with the possible exception of the letter

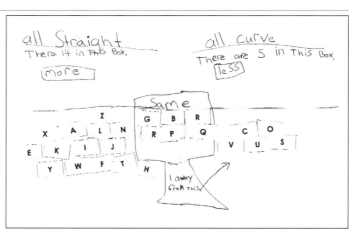

V. Jenna's work showed that she made observations of the number of letters in each of the groups and compared the groups. Jenna used comparative language to label the groups: the "all straight" letters have "more" (14 letters), the "all curve" letters have "less" (5 letters), and the mixed group has "1 away from" the "all curve" group (6 letters). She described the latter group not as *between* or in the *middle* but as "same," a response that required some inference on the part of the teacher.

Variations for the Range of Learners

To assist less-experienced students, the teacher may choose to limit the number of letters supplied or may ask students to select ten letters prior to giving the prompt. Using plastic or magnetic letters on a whiteboard rather than paper letters may be helpful for students who have less dexterity.

Students who have had more experience can be asked to sort the letters in a different way. For example, if their first display focused on the type of line used, they should use a different system of rules the second time (e.g., the number or type of "intersections" created by the lines).

> **Standard:** Develop and evaluate inferences and predictions that are based on data

Expectations
- Discuss events related to students' experiences as likely or unlikely
- Analyze events and communicate understanding to others

2

Is It Likely?

Grade range: Pre-K–2

About the mathematics: In the early grades, experiences with probability should invite students to make predictions about future events. The activities should be informal and related to the students' experiences to help them develop concepts of uncertainty. Initially those experiences should focus on the vocabulary of probability, using words such as *impossible, never, unlikely, likely, probably, maybe,* and *certain*. The "Is It Likely?" task asks students to determine how likely an event is and to place it in one of four categories—impossible, unlikely, likely, and certain—that represent an informal line of probability. In higher grades, such tasks use probability values from 0 to 1 instead of the designations contained on the informal line.

TASK

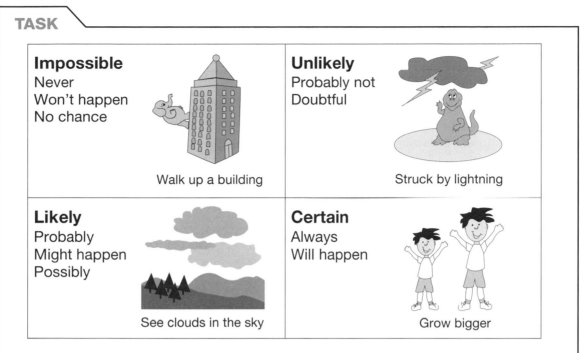

| **Impossible** Never Won't happen No chance *Walk up a building* | **Unlikely** Probably not Doubtful *Struck by lightning* |
| **Likely** Probably Might happen Possibly *See clouds in the sky* | **Certain** Always Will happen *Grow bigger* |

1. Place the category cards from left to right along the top of a table. Place the event cards in a stack, facedown.
2. Turn over an event card.
3. Is the event impossible, unlikely, likely, or certain? Put the event card where you think it fits best.
4. Why does it belong there?

Using this assessment task: Cut out the cards from the "Is it Likely? Category Cards" and "Is it Likely? Event Cards" blackline masters. The two blank cards can be used to create events that reflect the students' experience. Place the four category cards—impossible, unlikely, likely, and certain—from left to right along the top of a table. Additional words and an image are associated with the cards to assist those students who cannot yet read and those unfamiliar with the vocabulary. Working with small groups of two to four students, ensure that all the students are familiar with the four types of events prior to starting the task. The following are examples of the four types of events:

Impossible: It is impossible to walk up the side of a building.
Unlikely: It is unlikely that a person will get struck by lightning.
Likely: It is likely that you will see some clouds in the sky.
Certain: It is certain that you will grow bigger.

Once the students are familiar with the categories, place the event cards facedown on the table. Each student turns over an event card. Help students read their cards if necessary. Ask, "Is this event impossible, unlikely, likely, or certain?" If the student is not familiar with those words, the teacher may choose other words that are listed on the category cards. After the student places the card under a category, ask, "Why does it belong there?" Listen for the student's reasoning as he or she explains the likelihood of the event. Once the card has been placed under a category, ask the other students in the group whether they agree or disagree with the placement.

In addition to the event cards are four fill-in-the-blank cards. Students are to make up a future event and place it under one of the categories. Although all the cards say "I will …", students may make up events that will happen (e.g., tonight I will go to sleep), are likely to happen (e.g., tomorrow I will go to swimming), are unlikely to happen (e.g., in the morning I will have pizza for breakfast), or are impossible (e.g., next week I will fly to school). Once the students have made up an event, they are to place it under a category and justify their thinking.

Students in the early grades often mix fantasy and reality. Asking the students to explain why they placed the event under a particular category lends more insight into the evidence on which they have based their predictions. Frequently, making predictions based on fantasy does not mean that the student has not yet developed the underlying concept. Probing further may help the teacher assess the concept more thoroughly, for example, by asking, "How likely is it in real life? or "How likely is it that it will happen to you?"

Solution: The event cards were created to represent events under each category. However, depending on how the student justified his or her reasoning, answers may vary from those given in the following table. The teacher's interpretation is necessary to determine whether the student has appropriately justified placement for the teacher-created cards and for the fill-in-the-blank "I will …" cards.

Event Card	Category
It will snow tomorrow.	Unlikely, likely, or in some climates, perhaps impossible
You will have 2 birthdays this year.	Impossible, unless the student interprets the statement as meaning two birthday parties
A rock will sink when it is dropped into a glass of water.	Certain, except for pumice
The sky will be green tomorrow.	Impossible, unless the student lives where smog may give the sky a greenish hue
Everyone will be in class tomorrow.	Likely or unlikely, depending on the class
You will have spaghetti for supper.	Likely or unlikely, depending on the student
Touching fire will burn you.	Certain
You will read a book tonight.	Any category, depending on the student
There will be an elephant in your living room when you get home.	Impossible, unless the elephant is a toy
The spinner will land on red.	Unlikely, because the spinner has less red region than white

Continuum of Understanding

For each card drawn, record where the student placed the event card and the explanation given. Determine in which of the following categories the explanation and reasoning for the placement fall:

- *Unjustified or unreasonable:* does not offer an explanation or uses flawed reasoning
- *Partially justified:* reiterates the placement (e.g., "That's impossible") or uses language that does not fully match the placement (e.g., Certain: "It might happen")
- *Fully justified:* gives a clear and reasonable explanation

Looking for Evidence of Understanding

The table below presents a sample of responses from students across the grade span, from prekindergarten through second grade. The teacher recorded each student's placement and explanation, then evaluated each justification as being fully explained, partially explained, or unjustified or unreasonable.

Several students had difficulty with the vocabulary of *impossible* and *certain*. However, when other terminology was used, such as "never happens" or "always happens," all the children were able to offer appropriate justifications for most of their event-card placements.

Name	Card	Placement	Justification	Explanation
Ryan (pre-K)	2 Birthdays	Certain	Fully	"I always have two birthdays. A kids' birthday and then one with all the adults."
Sarah (K)	Rock	Certain	Fully	"'Cause rocks don't have air in them. Everything with air will float."
Ronan (Gr. 1)	Attendance	Likely	Fully	"Rosa was missing yesterday and today so she might be missing tomorrow too."
Karl (Gr. 1)	Fire	Likely	Fully	"My brother puts his hand through really fast and doesn't get burned. But I don't do it."
Alex (Gr. 1)	Book	Certain	Fully	"I read with my mom every night."
Tiera (K)	Next week I will	Impossible	Fully	"This is a silly one. Next week I will kiss my friend. I wouldn't really do that."
Kyle (Gr. 1)	Tomorrow I will	Certain	Fully	"Tomorrow I'll have a hamburger when I go to Earl's for my birthday."
MacKenzie (K)	Tonight I will	Likely	Fully	"Tonight I might listen to music on the microphone. I usually do that."
Stella (Gr. 2)	In the morning I will	Certain	Fully	"In the morning I will have cereal for breakfast. I always have cereal."
Noah (pre-K)	Snow	Certain	Partially	"I think it will snow." [Snow was falling the day this activity took place.]
Olivia (K)	Green sky	Impossible	Partially	"That would never happen."
Josh (K)	Spaghetti	Certain	Partially	"I like spaghetti." Teacher: "But do you have it every night?" "No, but I think tonight we will."
Sarah (K)	Spinner	Likely	Partially	"The spinner doesn't always land on one color. Unless it is unfair." [Sarah did not take into account that the red region is only one-fourth of the spinner.]
Erin (pre-K)	Elephant	Likely	Unjustified	Teacher asked, "Do you think that would happen in real life?" Erin shrugged her shoulders and nodded yes.

Variations for the Range of Learners

The teacher should choose event cards that are suitable for the particular groups of students. This consideration may mean eliminating some cards and creating additional cards. For example, the spinner card may be eliminated if it is not familiar to students.

Less-experienced students may have difficulty categorizing the cards into four categories. As an alternative, the teacher may choose to create three categories: impossible, possible, and certain. In the "possible" category, include additional vocabulary, such as *might happen* or *maybe*. Inexperienced students may also have difficulty creating events for the fill-in-the-blank cards. If so, those cards can be eliminated. More-experienced students can be challenged to place the events along a continuum from impossible to certain rather than place them into categories.

Standard: Develop and evaluate inferences and predictions that are based on data

Expectations
- Discuss events related to students' experiences as likely or unlikely
- Use reasoning to make predictions
- Use representations to model mathematical phenomena
- Communicate mathematical thinking to others

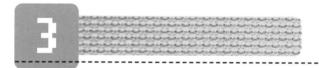

Prediction Game

Grade range: Pre-K–2

About the mathematics: The "Prediction Game" task assesses initial understandings of probability and prediction strategies in a game format. Two trials of the game are played, in which the players predict one of two possible events before their turn. For example, they may predict that a green card will be turned over. Teachers can use this task to assess students' intuitive sense of chance and determine whether they change their strategy for winning the game after becoming aware of the number of cards of each color involved.

TASK

Players: Two players participate (i.e., student and teacher), but only one player makes the predictions.

Setup: Shuffle ten cards, and place them on the table facing down. Some cards are green, and some are yellow.

Play: Before each card is turned over, predict which color you think the card will be. Record the prediction. If you are correct, you get one counter. If you are incorrect, the other person gets one counter. Whoever has the most counters at the end of the game wins.

Think back: After the first game is played, look at the cards. What strategy will you use to play the game a second time? Why do you think that strategy will help you? Play the game again. Did your strategy work?

Using this assessment task: This task is written so that it can be used one-on-one with students, particularly in the younger age range. However, it can be easily adapted for pairs of students. The task requires a set of ten cards. One side of the cards should be either green or yellow, and the other side should be left blank. Use the ratio of 8:2 or 7:3 to ensure that one color dominates. For example, the card set should contain eight green cards and two yellow cards, making very likely the outcome that a green card is turned over. In that version of the game, only one student makes predictions for all ten cards.

If cards are not available, a set of ten objects that are identical in size and shape can be used (e.g., tiles, clothespins, blocks, etc.). The objects should differ by one attribute, for example, be of two different colors or have two different pictures, words, or symbols on them. If you use objects, ensure that the attributes are hidden by having students draw the objects from a concealed bag.

Additional materials required for the task include counters and a sheet of paper for recording predictions. A sheet of paper prepared in advance with the numbers 1 to 10 may be useful to allow the teacher to record the predictions for each of the ten trials using the words, symbols, or colors. Keep the predictions visible as the student plays the game.

As students play the game the first time, many of them will notice that one color occurs more frequently than the other. If they do not appear to notice the results after the first game, encourage students to spread out all ten objects, and ask what they notice about the objects and how they might use that information to help create a strategy for the next time they play the game.

In the first game, the teacher should notice how often each color was predicted and in what order. Older children often systematically switch back and forth between the two colors. Younger children may consistently pick their favorite color or choose more randomly. The first game furnishes a baseline to determine how the student makes his or her predictions. Once students become aware of the number of objects of each color involved, assess whether they predict the dominant color more often in the second game. For example, if a student has systematically picked five green and five yellow cards in the first game, the teacher looks for whether the student chooses more green than yellow cards in the second game. Whether the student wins or scores more or fewer points in the second round is not important.

Solution: The teacher may see the following results for a student who has recognized the predominance of green cards over yellow cards:

Trial	1	2	3	4	5	6	7	8	9	10	Predictions
Game 1	Y	Y	G	G	Y	Y	G	Y	G	Y	6 Y 4 G

Teacher. "In the first game, you predicted six yellow and four green. What strategy will you use the second time?"
Student. "There were lots more green, so I'm going to pick green at the beginning."

Game 2	G	G	Y	G	Y	G	G	Y	Y	G	4 Y 6 G

Teacher. "Did your strategy work?"
Student. "Sort of. I lost last time and tied this time."

The student predicted green more often in the second game. Although the student may not have won game 2, she was aware that the chances of green were more likely and so had shifted her prediction toward a more frequent choice of green.

Continuum of Understanding

Subjective Understanding

- Does not notice the predominance of one attribute over another, with or without prompting; is unable to use the information to state or use a strategy in the second game; continues to use subjective means (e.g., favorite color) to make predictions or may continue to systematically alternate between the two choices
- Predicts the dominant color the same number of times or perhaps fewer times than in the previous game

Developing Understanding

- May not notice that one color occurs more often than another until prompted; may use that information to state a strategy but does not use that strategy consistently in the second game
- Predicts the dominant color as often as, or slightly more often than, in the first game

Strong Understanding

- During or at the end of the first game, becomes aware without prompting that one attribute occurs more often; uses that information to state a strategy, and employs that strategy to the extent that the number of predictions favors the dominant attribute in the second game; may also adjust predictions at the end of the second game on the basis of knowing how many objects with each attribute remain
- Predicts the dominant color more frequently in the second game

Looking for Evidence of Understanding

Many of the prekindergarten students were able to develop clear strategies for the second game after looking at the number of cards of each color. If eight green and two yellow cards were involved, many students were able to keep track of the number of yellows that had occurred and used that information during the game to make predictions. That is, if two yellow cards had appeared by the seventh card, the student picked green for the remaining three cards.

Tara: Subjective Understanding

Drawing purple and orange sticks from a bag, Tara predicted five purple and five orange sticks randomly in the first game. On completion, she did not notice that eight purple sticks were involved. With the sticks in front of her, she was asked what strategy she might use in the second game. She said, "I don't know. It's hard to guess, but I like orange." In the second game she picked only four purple sticks and six orange sticks.

Sarah: Developing Understanding

For a set of cards having seven blue cards and three red cards, Sarah predicted five blue and five red cards randomly in the first game. At the end of the game, she was prompted to look at the cards, and she counted of the number of each color involved. She said, "It's likely you would get blues, not reds." However, she did not use that information for the second game until the end, as shown in the teacher's written record of her predictions. She alternated between red and blue until the seventh card. The third red card appeared as the ninth turned-over card, and at that point she said, "This last one I have to pick blue because I know there are only three reds."

Name: Sarah	
Game 1	Game 2
1. Blue	1. Red
2. Blue	2. Blue
3. Red	3. Red
4. Red	4. Blue
5. Blue	5. Red
6. Red	6. Red
7. Red	7. Blue
8. Red	8. Blue
9. Blue	9. Blue
10. Blue	10. Blue
5 Blue 5 Red	6 Blue 4 Red

Noah: Strong Understanding

Noah alternated between green and yellow for the first half of the first game and noticed that more greens had appeared, so he picked predominantly greens in the second half of the game. The deck contained two yellow cards and eight green cards. After looking at the cards, he said, "There are more green and only two yellows." The strategy that he stated for the second game was "Only say two yellows." Although he did not use that strategy, at the end of the second game he said, "I was always guessing green because I knew I would only get two wrong."

Variations for the Range of Learners

Although the activity involves only two trials of the game, students with limited experience may benefit from conducting several trials. They may then begin to realize that they will be more successful if they choose the dominant attribute more frequently.

When playing with two players, include twenty cards so that each person makes ten predictions. Use an 8-to-2 ratio (i.e., sixteen of one attribute and four of another). Each student takes a turn predicting the attribute, recording his or her own prediction, and selecting an object. If the prediction is correct, he or she receives one counter. If he or she is incorrect, the partner receives the counter. An added challenge is to keep the objects hidden once they have been selected. That version of the game requires students to realize during the game that one attribute occurs more frequently than the other rather than allows them to count the number of objects with each attribute at the end of the first game.

Standard: Formulate questions that can be addressed with data and collect, organize, and display relevant data to answer them

Expectations

- Pose questions about themselves and their surroundings
- Organize and consolidate their mathematical thinking through communication

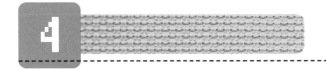

I Wonder

Grade range: K–2

About the mathematics: In this task students are asked to formulate questions about people or objects in their surroundings and to identify data-collection strategies, such as making an observation, taking a survey, or doing an experiment, that could be used to answer the questions. Students should be encouraged to focus on questions involving two (or more) categories of comparison. They are not required to answer the questions they pose in this assessment task, but the teacher may want to offer the opportunity for them to do so. Questions generated by the students are motivating and give students a purpose for gathering, analyzing, and presenting data.

TASK

1. Look around the classroom. In it are students, books, bins, desks, and many other things. Create a question that you don't know the answer to, and use words or pictures to fill in the blanks in the following sentence:

   Are there more _____ or _____ in our classroom?

2. How could you find an answer to your question?

Using this assessment task: This task is designed to be used with the whole class. Children who have not learned to write yet may need extra assistance to script their responses. Each student will need a blank sheet of paper and writing or drawing tools. The teacher may want to write the prompt on chart paper or on the board.

The task as written is structured so that students ask questions that compare two or more categories. Some students may ask good, but noncomparative, questions, such as "How many desks are there in the room?" or "How many years has Mrs. Sharpe been a teacher?" Encourage students to focus on the prompt and to ask questions to which they do not already know the answer. Some students may need examples before they can pose appropriate questions. Possible questions to pose include "Are there more students wearing long sleeves or short sleeves?" "Are there more people who like dogs or cats?" and "Are there more red blocks or blue blocks in this bin?"

The second part of the question asks students to describe a way to collect and record the data. Additional prompting may be needed to get detailed answers. If a student says he will count the number of students wearing long sleeves and short sleeves, for example, you may want to ask, "How will you keep track?" or "How can you make sure you've counted everyone only once?"

Solution: An appropriate solution is one that poses a question in which two or more categories are compared. Students should be able to communicate appropriate data-collection strategies for the questions posed.

Sample Solution
- Question: "Are there more people who like juice or milk?"
- Data-collection strategy: "I'll make a chart with juice and milk. Then I'll ask everyone what they like, and I'll mark it on my chart."

Continuum of Understanding

Not Yet Started
- Gives no response
- Asks a question that is not answerable through data collection
- Is not able to identify strategies or plans that could be used to collect data to answer the question posed

Developing Understanding
- Poses a question that is not easily answerable through data-collection strategies, or poses noncomparative questions
- Identifies strategies or plans that may be difficult to use, or supplies incomplete or inaccurate data to answer the question

Secure Understanding

- Suggests a question that is easily answerable through data-collection strategies
- Identifies strategies or plans that could be used to collect data to answer the question, and communicates a means to account for all the data

Looking for Evidence of Understanding

Teachers might consider making "I wonder" part of a daily routine. For example, one teacher included this task as part of her daily directed-learning time. Initially, she modeled the questions and data-collection strategies for the students. With practice, the students became able to suggest appropriate questions and to select and use a variety of methods for data collection. Discussions of the data prompt the use of mathematical language and comparisons.

Not Yet Started

Students who are unable to furnish evidence of understanding may experience difficulty generating questions and so offer statements instead. Those who are able to frame questions may suggest questions for which only one response is possible, for example, may ask, "What day is it today?" or "Is it raining outside?"

Kevin: Developing Understanding

Kevin initially posed a non-comparative question that was not easily answerable: "Is there more paper in the classroom?" The teacher prompted the use of the stem, "Is there more ___ or ___?" to frame a question, and Kevin was then able to pose a comparative question: "Are there more oranges or apples in the classroom?" Kevin identified a data-collection strategy that may or may not have been efficient or effective: "By eating them." He made no mention of counting or recording the data.

Kiera: Secure Understanding

Kiera first posed a comparative question that referred to paper and projects that were on display in her classroom. The question was easily answerable. Her second question was also a comparative question that referred to observable data. With respect to possible strategies for answering both questions, Kiera identified counting as an appropriate method for data collection and sug-

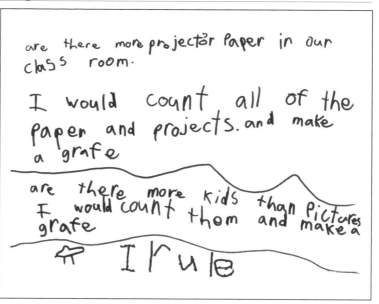

gested the use of a graph for organizing and displaying the data once they were collected.

Variations for the Range of Learners

To assist students who have limited experience, restrict the variety of objects about which they can pose their questions. Bins of items typically used for sorting are a good starting point (e.g., buttons, shells, or a junk box).

Students with more experience may not need the fill-in-the-blank prompt. Ask those students to pose questions that compare people or objects in the classroom and to state a method that they could use to find an answer using familiar data-collection strategies. This more open-ended task may encourage students to make comparisons among more than two objects.

Standards
- Formulate questions that can be addressed with data and collect, organize, and display relevant data to answer them
- Select and use appropriate statistical methods to analyze data

Expectations
- Pose questions and gather data about themselves and their surroundings
- Represent data using concrete objects, pictures, and graphs
- Describe parts of the data and the set of data as a whole to determine what the data show
- Create and use representations to organize, record, and communicate mathematical ideas
- Use the language of mathematics to express mathematical ideas

5

What Is Your Favorite?

Grade range: K–2

About the mathematics: The "What Is Your Favorite?" task assesses the four stages of the data-analysis process: posing a question (parts 1 and 2), collecting data (part 3), displaying data (part 4), and interpreting the results (part 5). Students choose a topic that is familiar and of interest to them and generate possible responses so as to limit the respondents' choices and simplify the recording. They are expected to collect data and organize those data using a format of their choosing and to describe and interpret the data collected.

TASK

1. **Pose a question:** "What is your favorite _____?" What are six different ways you could finish your question? Choose one that is interesting to you.

2. **Think about possible answers:** What do you think will be the most popular answers to your question? Choose three.

3. **Collect data:** Ask your classmates how they would answer the question, given the three choices you have provided. Keep a record of their answers.

4. **Organize the data:** Organize the answers, and show your results.

5. **Interpret the data:** What does your display tell you about the results?

Using this assessment task: This task is designed for use with the whole class. The teacher will need to give instructions at the beginning of each stage in the task. The entire process may occur over two or three days to ensure that students have sufficient time to brainstorm ideas and to collect data.

For parts 1 and 2 of the task, use a blank sheet of paper folded in half. On the left side students record their ideas for possible questions, and on the right side they generate possible responses. Suggest possible questions for students who have difficulty starting the task, for example, What is your favorite ice cream, color, hockey team, animal? Students brainstorm possible responses to their selected questions and choose only three. Restricting participants' responses to a selection of one of three options limits the results to three possibilities.

In parts 3 and 4, provide students with paper, cubes, sticky notes, grid paper, linking cubes, and other materials for the data-collection and organization stages. Allow students to collect and record their own data and to organize them in a format of their choosing. For example, for collecting data, they could use tally marks, check marks, objects, or pictures to represent each person's choice. For organizing the data, they could use an object graph, a picture graph, a bar graph, or a tally chart to display their results. If students have limited experience collecting data independently, the teacher may provide additional support. Students can be given a class list or a chart labeled "Name" and "Answer" to assist them with data collection. Similarly, the teacher may supply grid paper or a bar-graph outline and prompt students to include a title and labels on the display of the results. Although the number of students who should be surveyed is not specified, the teacher may recommend that students survey at least ten people.

Part 5 is open-ended. The expectation is that students will be able to identify which response occurred most often and least often using numerical comparisons. Some prompting may be required to make such comparisons.
Solution: Parts 1 and 2: What is your favorite ____? What are three likely responses?

Examples

Sport: soccer, hockey, swimming
Candy: candy bar, lollipop, licorice
Animal: dog, cat, horse

Part 3: Data collection may involve the following components:

- A list of responses in the order given
- A chart identifying the three choices and a tally given for each response
- The respondent's name and his or her choice

Examples

Soccer	ⅢⅢ ⅢⅢ
Hockey	|||
Swimming	||||

Jaimie	Soccer
Kiera	Swimming
Justin	Soccer
Sean	Hockey

Part 4: The organization of the data may be accomplished with one of the following:

- Bar graph
- Picture graph
- Object graph
- Tally chart
- Objects, pictures, or names sorted into three distinct groups

The student should also include a title and labels on the selected organizational device.

Example: What is your favorite sport?

Soccer	⚽	⚽	⚽	⚽	⚽
Hockey	🏒	🏒			
Swimming	🏊	🏊	🏊	🏊	

Part 5: Interpret results

Students should make comparisons among categories using the terms *most* and *least* or numerical comparisons. The following are sample responses:

Most people liked soccer the best. Swimming second best. Hockey the least. Five people liked soccer. Two people liked hockey. Four people liked swimming. One more person liked soccer compared with swimming.

Continuum of Understanding

	Needs More Experience	**Developing**	**On Target**
Pose a question	Has difficulty posing questions that would be appropriate for a survey; is unable to identify possible responses other than his or her own	Once prompted, is able to pose two to three questions and provide two to three possible responses	Has little difficulty independently posing at least three ideas and at least three possible responses
Collect data	Requires ongoing assistance to collect data	Requires some assistance to initiate data collection; may need a teacher-suggested strategy to complete the data collection; makes generally accurate recordings	Works independently to collect data, and creates a record that allows him or her to accurately capture respondents' responses
Organize data	Uses a teacher-provided method for displaying the data, but produces an incomplete graph or makes several errors in transferring the data	Requires assistance to organize and display the data; may need prompting by the teacher to use a particular method; may require a teacher-supplied framework for displaying the data	Chooses an appropriate way to organize data; accurately transfers responses to the display; provides useful information, such as a title, labels, and categories, as well as a means to identify the frequency
Interpret results	Is unable to make appropriate interpretations of the results	Is able to identify which choice occurs most often or least often using words or pictures; makes no numerical comparisons of the data	Is able to identify which response occurred most often and which occurred least often using words or pictures; uses numerical comparisons

Looking for Evidence of Understanding

In the early grades students are not expected to distinguish between a sample and a population. Although most students engaging in this task will be surveying only a sample of their classmates, they may, as Alek and Stephie did, refer to "everyone" and "most people." These and other students who did the task were referring only to the students they surveyed. However, asking them whether their results would be true if they surveyed the whole class or the whole school would be useful to promote meaningful discussion.

Alek

Pose a question: On Target

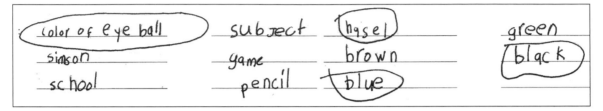

Alek had little difficulty generating six ideas for questions. After selecting and circling "color of eye ball" as his survey question, he independently generated possible colors and chose three: hazel, blue, and black.

Collect data: Developing
Alek surveyed seven classmates and used tallies to record their responses. However, he viewed the survey as a win-lose game and was overheard asking respondents to switch their response to hazel–his own eye color.

Organize data: Developing

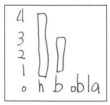

Alek used a bar chart similar to that being used by other students around him. He accurately transferred the data to the chart. He labeled the categories (h, b, bla) and frequency axes; however, he did not give a title to the chart.

Interpret results: Developing
In keeping with "winning," Alek incorrectly wrote that everyone liked hazel better and then said he had finished. After being prompted to write how many of each color had been selected, he wrote further comparisons.

[Everyone likes hazel better than blue and black. Hazel won. Black lost. 4 people liked hazel. 3 people liked blue. 0 people liked black.]

evryone likes hasel better then blue and black. hasel won black lost. 4 people liked hasel 3 people liked blue o people liked black.

Stephie

Pose a question: On Target

Stephie generated several possible questions. After choosing "dog," she listed five types of dogs and chose three: weimaraner, German shepherd, and golden retriever.

Collect data: On Target

Stephie independently created a bar graph and tally chart prior to collecting her data.

Organize data: On Target

Stephie created four representations of the data. She made a minor error in one representation, in which she included an extra tally mark. She clearly understood different representations and labeled them appropriately, but she did not include any titles.

Interpret results: On Target

Stephie identified the most and least frequent responses, and although she did not state how many responses were in the largest group, she noted that the two smallest groups had one each.

Variations for the Range of Learners

As indicated throughout the task, students with limited experience may need a variety of prompts and frameworks to be able to complete the task successfully. The teacher may choose to limit the task to two possible responses rather than three and to offer a structured approach to collecting and displaying data by preparing a class list and a picture-graph outline in advance. More-experienced students do not need to be limited to three responses and can survey the whole class.

Standard: Develop and evaluate inferences and predictions that are based on data

Expectations

- Discuss events related to students' experiences as likely or unlikely
- Develop mathematical arguments
- Communicate their mathematical thinking coherently and clearly to others

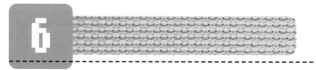

Is It Fair?

Grade range: K–2

About the mathematics: In this task students are asked to think about probability as it relates to a six-sided colored cube. The task assesses whether students understand, at least informally, the concept that the act of rolling a cube is a random event and that each color is equally likely to occur. The format for this task is a game. Students are asked to articulate whether the color choice for the "start" of the game matters. Students with subjective notions of probability typically view their favorite color as being the most likely and the most fair.

My friend and I were playing a game that used a colored cube. The cube had a different color on each face. One face was red, one blue, one yellow, one green, one black, and one orange.

To go, first you need to roll a green.

My friend said, "That's not fair! We should roll yellow to start, not green."

Do you think rolling green first is fair? Why or why not?

Using this assessment task: This task is designed for use with the whole class. The teacher explains the scenario to the class and asks the students to individually write or state whether they think starting with green is fair. The students should justify their thinking. They need to be familiar with games that use dice or colored cubes. Supplying students with colored cubes is optional, but doing so changes the task in that it allows students to test their ideas prior to responding.

Solution: The correct solution is one in which a student says that first rolling green or yellow—or any other color—is fair. A student with strong understanding will realize that each color is equally likely to be rolled. The notion of "equally likely" is a sophisticated concept. Sufficient understanding for this task is the realization that any of the six colors can be used to start the game; which color is chosen does not matter.

Continuum of Understanding

Limited Reasoning

- May choose fair or not fair but be unable to articulate his or her reasoning
- May base a decision on her or his favorite color or on the color that is rolled, that is, having rolled orange, may say, "I think it should be orange."

Developing Reasoning

- Indicates that green is fair, and may state that it doesn't matter if it is green or yellow but be unable to articulate the reasoning behind the choice

Adequate Reasoning

- Indicates that either green or yellow is fair; offers evidence of understanding that rolling the dice is random and that the choice of color used to start the game does not matter—any of the six colors would be fair.

Strong Reasoning

- Indicates that because each of the six colors is shown once, each color is equally likely, so any color chosen is fair; in fact, a different color could be chosen prior to each person's roll.

Looking for Evidence of Understanding

Many children related the fairness of the scenario to the selection of the color ("green is go and yellow is slow" or "green means go on a traffic light, so it is fair"). Many students did not make the connection between fairness and the likelihood or probability of rolling green as compared with rolling any of the other colors on the cube. Teachers may wish to repeat the task, selecting a different color as the target for the game scenario to illustrate that the color choice does not matter.

Teddy: Limited Reasoning

Teddy indicated that "if everybody gets the same color, then the youngest should go first." His response did not relate to rolling the die or the fairness of rolling one of the colors on the die. In a similar fashion, his classmate Ashlee indicated that "it is not really fair and it would be nice to let someone else go first if they don't know how to play."

Gary: Adequate Reasoning

> It is fair Because you Don't Know what you are going to get.

Gary's response indicated an awareness that the outcome from rolling a die is random. Gary was able to relate the concept of fairness to the fact that the possible outcomes, such as rolling green with the die, are obtained by chance.

Ivan: Strong Reasoning

> Yes! Because Green comes up the same times as Yellow only lots of times about; 150 times I think!

Ivan's response indicated an awareness that the results of rolling a die are random; fairness is determined on the basis of the randomness of the event (e.g., rolling green). Ivan also showed evidence of understanding that the probability of rolling either green or yellow is theoretically the same but that many trials ("150 times I think!") would be required before the results would match.

Variations for the Range of Learners

The teacher may choose other objects typically used in games to make the task either more or less challenging. Tossing a coin (two outcomes) or using a four-color spinner (four outcomes) will simplify the task. Students who are less familiar with equally likely events may be asked to roll the cube (or spin the spinner) several times while keeping track of the results to provide them with some experience on which to base and justify their reasoning.

Standards
- Formulate questions that can be addressed with data and collect, organize, and display relevant data to answer them
- Select and use appropriate statistical methods to analyze data
- Develop and evaluate inferences and predictions that are based on data

Expectations
- Sort and classify objects according to their attributes and organize data about the objects
- Gather data through experiments
- Represent data using concrete objects, pictures, and graphs
- Describe parts of the data and the set of data as a whole to determine what the data show
- Discuss events related to students' experiences as likely or unlikely
- Communicate reasoning
- Use representations to organize, record, and communicate mathematical ideas

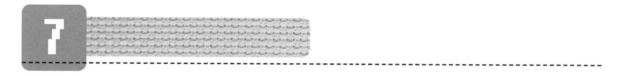

Picking Possibilities

Grade range: K–2

About the mathematics: This task incorporates many of the expectations in data analysis and probability. However, the focus of the assessment is on identifying combinations and interpreting the results of an experiment. Students are first asked to determine the possible combinations of two objects with two possible colors. They then conduct an experiment of ten trials by picking two objects at a time out of a bag, recording the results, and returning the objects to the bag. The bag contains sticks of two different colors, with decidedly more of one color than the other, increasing the likelihood of a particular combination. As students conduct the experiment and organize their results, many will notice that one color predominates. When asked to interpret the results, students should indicate which color pair occurs most often. At the end, students may be able to hypothesize why one particular color combination dominated over the other possible combinations.

TASK

Understand: I put some red and blue tiles in the bag. If I asked you to reach in and pick two tiles out of the bag, what colors might the tiles be? Draw or write the possible combinations.

Experiment: Pick 2 tiles from the bag. Record the color for each tile. Put the tiles back in the bag. Repeat this process 10 times. Keep a record of your results.

Interpret: Which color pairs are most likely? Least likely? Why do you think so?

Using this assessment task: The "Picking Possibilities" task is designed to be used with small groups. The experiment portion of the task can be done within the small-group configuration so that all members of the group have the same results.

The materials needed for the task include objects of the same size and shape but of two different colors (e.g., craft sticks, colored clothespins, colored tiles) and a bag or an opaque bucket. In the bag place five objects of one color and fifteen objects of another color. Give each student several objects in the corresponding colors and a copy of the "Picking Possibilities" blackline master.

Students who have limited experience determining possible combinations may require assistance in part 1 of the task. The teacher may need to present an example by reaching into the bag and pulling out one possible combination. Many students will need to determine the combinations using the sticks first, followed by drawing their results or having their responses recorded. In this task, a red-blue combination is considered the same as a blue-red combination; however, in part 1, students may record them as different. If students have difficulty determining how to record their results or how to organize them, prompt a discussion of whether red-blue can be considered the same as blue-red to simplify the task.

Once students have completed the ten trials, focus their attention on the interpretation questions (part 4). A place to organize the results of the experiment is provided on the blackline master (part 3), but the student may not need to use that space to answer the questions. If the student struggles, the teacher may suggest using a tally chart to organize the results.

Most students can easily identify the "most likely" combination, but if one combination did not occur at all in the ten trials, students may not realize that it is least likely. The teacher may need to suggest that students review the possible combinations identified in part 1. When asking students to interpret why some combinations were more likely or less likely than others, the teacher may need to prompt them by asking, "What do you think is in the bag?" or "How many of each color do you think are in the bag?"

Solution: The following solution is based on using fifteen blue sticks and five red sticks.

Understand: The three combinations are (1) blue-blue, (2) blue-red (or red-blue), and (3) red-red.

Experiment: If the sample contains fifteen blue sticks and five red sticks, students may record the trials using colored pictures, symbols, words (e.g., blue, red), or initials (e.g., B or R) to identify the different colors. The teacher should expect to see predominantly blue-blue combinations followed by blue-red combinations, with very few, if any, red-red combinations.

Organize results: Students may or may not use the space provided to help them organize the results of the experiment. Organization may take the form of tally charts, bar graphs, or a sorting and reordering of the trials. The following chart is an example:

Blue–Blue	ⵑⵑ I
Blue–Red	III
Red–Red	I

Interpret: Numerical answers may vary, but blue-blue is most likely combination, followed by blue-red. The least likely is red-red.

Continuum of Understanding

	1	2	3
Combinations	Is unable to determine possible combinations after prompting	Is able to identify three (or four) combinations with some prompting (e.g., the teacher provides one combination)	Is able to identify the three (or four) combinations without prompting
Experiment	Is unable to keep records of the trials	Initially requires assistance with record keeping but is able to do it independently by the fifth trial	Correctly records the ten trials using pictures, words, or symbols
Interpret	Has difficulty identifying *most often* and *least often;* may be unable to find a means to count or organize the trials in a way that helps make a distinction; is unable to infer what is in the bag even after prompting	Correctly identifies the combination that occurs most often and the one that occurs least often, but may need some prompting on *least often* if one combination did not occur	From the results of the experiment, correctly identifies the combination that occurs most often and the one that occurs least often; is also able to infer that the results likely indicate that more of one color than the other is present

Looking for Evidence of Understanding

Shea: Score 1-1-1

Shea was not able to identify the possible combinations. She kept saying that yellow and green were the only possibilities because those were the color of the sticks. She was not able to interpret the results of the experiment: "Most likely is yellow because it's so bright ... green's not very good. I don't like dark green." She drew lines to match

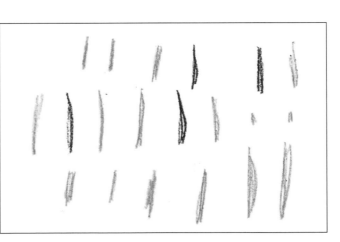

the colors of the sticks as they were drawn from the bag but did not organize or track the number of trials. She observed that she was "getting more yellows and more greens and yellows" midway through the experiment.

Rachel: Score 2-2-1

Rachel was unclear at first but then easily and confidently offered three possibilities. Shea directed the recording, which was done by the teacher. Shea counted to track the number of trials, and she commented on the results during the experiment. Her teacher recorded the results of each trial and the dialogue between teacher and student during the experiment. The squiggly marks on the sheet are Shea's attempt to count how many of each combination resulted, but the method she used was not consistent. Shea stated, "Red is most often." Because she did not have a method for counting accurately or keeping track, Shea's interpretations were inconsistent with the actual results.

Josh: Score 3-3-3

Josh was able to identify the three possible combinations. He also accurately recorded and organized both the results of the trials and the results of the experiment. Josh correctly identified the combinations that were most and least likely on the basis of his recorded results. He inferred from the results of the experiment that the sample contained a greater proportion of yellow sticks.

Variations for the Range of Learners

Students with considerable experience may be able to identify the possible combinations for sticks of three different colors. This capability may occur after the task with two colors has been completed, or the teacher may choose to have the students do the entire task with three different colors. If the latter version is chosen, be careful to ensure that one color predominates. The predominance of one color will allow students to make appropriate interpretations in part 3.

If students are unable to identify possible combinations in part 1, the teacher may show the three possible combinations to the students so that they can concentrate on organizing the results. The teacher may need to help some students with organizing the results of the ten trials, for instance, by supplying a template of a tally chart or a color graph. Such assistance may provide enough structure to allow students to make appropriate interpretations in part 3.

Standard: Select and use appropriate statistical methods to analyze data

Expectations
- Describe parts of the data and the set of data as a whole to determine what the data show
- Communicate mathematical thinking to others

8

Do You Have All the Information You Need?

Grade range: 1–2

About the mathematics: In this age of communication and technology, children are constantly being bombarded with data and advertising. Having the skills and knowledge to interpret all the data to which they are exposed is crucial if children are to make wise decisions. In this task students are asked to make sense of an incomplete representation of a data set. This open-ended question fosters insight into how well students understand and interpret data. The task presents an opportunity for students to raise appropriate statistical questions. Will students formulate a question that might furnish a topic and title for this graph? The data state that students in a second-grade class made the graph but do not indicate how many students were involved. Will students question how many children were in the class? Will they question the types of possible labels that could be given to each column on the graph? After suggesting a topic or title for the graph, will the students question whether the labels for each column coincide with the topic and the title?

TASK

A group of second graders made this graph. It tells you something about their class.

What might the graph tell you about this class?

What information is missing that would help you find out about the class?

Using this assessment task: Give each student a copy of the "Do You Have All the Information You Need?" blackline master. Read the instructions together, and then allow students to examine the incomplete graph independently and record their ideas. Encourage students to generate several ideas about the graph and what it might represent. Assure students that the graph may represent many different scenarios. Students will need previous experience with graphs to be able to identify the missing components, such as the title and column labels. Some students will benefit from teacher prompts as they consider what type of data is represented. If the students hesitate in responding, a suggest that they look around the classroom to see what information is contained in the graphs that are being displayed. The teacher may also furnish an example of a scenario that this graph could be representing, for example, how students in the class get to school. If that had been the question posed, students could then be prompted to supply a title, for instance, "How Do You Get to School?" and also labels for each column—Walk, Bus, Car. Once the students are comfortable working through a guided example of a graph with missing elements, encourage them to suggest a different scenario that the same graph might represent.

Solution: The missing aspects of the graph include labels for each of the categories, a title, and perhaps the frequency of each category. The graph can have many interpretations, but the number of categories is limited to three. The following are examples:

- How many books did the child read in the last month? 0, 1, or 2
- What kind of ice cream do children like? Chocolate, Strawberry, Vanilla
- What color of eyes do the children have? Brown, Blue, Hazel

Students should recognize comparisons among the different categories, that is, the first was selected by five respondents, the second by eight, and the third by two. The second category is the most frequent or most popular. Knowing the number of respondents that chose each category also enables some students to calculate that fifteen people participated.

Continuum of Understanding

Limited Understanding

- Does not recognize the figure as a graph
- May count the happy faces but not be able to communicate what the faces might represent

Developing Understanding

- Notices that the graph has three parts
- Notices that the middle column has the most icons and the third column has the least
- States with prompting that information is missing and that labels or a title are missing
- May not be able to give an example of what the graph might represent

Strong Understanding

- Correctly counts the number of icons in each column: five, eight, and two; is able to make numerical comparisons among the columns
- Indicates that fifteen happy faces are present, so probably fifteen students are in the class or fifteen people participated
- Is able to give an example of what the graph might reference
- Is able to state that column labels and a title would help an observer understand the graph

Looking for Evidence of Understanding

Students in the early grades usually have had some experiences with graphing. However, unless prompted, many students do not attempt to make use of the quantities for comparisons that would help them interpret the graph more thoroughly.

Amy: Limited Understanding

After reading the "Do You Have All the information You Need?" student sheet together with the teacher, Amy sat quietly looking at the page. When the teacher asked, "What do you think?" Amy shrugged her shoulders. The teacher then asked her, "What kinds of graphs have you done in your class?" Amy drew a picture of a simple network and said, "We've done things like that" and then erased her work. The teacher asked, "What might help you make sense of this?" She said, "You could put them highest to lowest" and wrote "highest to lowest" on her page. Amy appeared to have had limited experience with graphing.

Emma: Developing Understanding

Emma asked if she could redraw the graph because "drawing helps me think." She correctly copied the number of happy faces to the new graph and said that the graph "shows what people like to do in winter." She made some nonnumerical comparisons verbally: "Most people like to build snowmen" and "Not very many like to build forts." She did not indicate what information was missing, nor did she make numerical comparisons.

Alex: Strong Understanding

> there ote No. labels
>
> The one with 2 people will be
> people who are writing. The
> (has 8)
> biggest group of people will be
> people who are drawing. The
> group with 5 people in it are the
> group that made this ~~shape~~ graph.
> Start with writing then go to drawing.
> Last group is done both.
> There is 15 people in the class

Alex quickly realized and wrote "there are no labels" and then asked the teacher to write down the rest of his response. For his example, he described the number of people at each phase in a project: writing, drawing, or both. He was careful to indicate how many people were in each phase and the relative size of the group. On completion, he counted the faces and indicated the total number of people.

Variations for the Range of Learners

This task can be modified by decreasing the number of pieces that are missing from the graph. For example, the teacher might add a title, such as "What Is Your Favorite Sport?" but omit the column labels. Alternatively, additional columns can be added to the chart to make the task more challenging for students.

Standards
- Formulate questions that can be addressed with data and collect, organize, and display relevant data to answer them
- Develop and evaluate inferences and predictions that are based on data

Expectations
- Gather and organize data about themselves and their surroundings
- Discuss events related to students' experiences as likely or unlikely
- Create and use representations to organize, record, and communicate mathematical ideas
- Communicate mathematical thinking to others
- Make and investigate mathematical conjectures

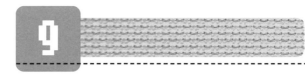

Paper-Clip Spin

Grade range: 1–2

About the mathematics: In the "Paper-Clip Spin" task, students conduct a simple probability experiment and record the results of the experiment. The task helps the teacher assess students' understanding of probability and their ability to organize and record data. The task requires students to develop a plan to effectively address the task and select an efficient method for recording the data collected. Students are then asked to use the data and apply their understanding of chance to make a reasonable prediction of possible outcomes if the experiment was to be repeated.

TASK

You are going to do an experiment by spinning a paper clip around the point of your pencil.

Spinner: Put a paper clip on the table in front of you. Put your pencil inside one of the ends of the paper clip. Use your finger to spin the paper clip around the pencil.

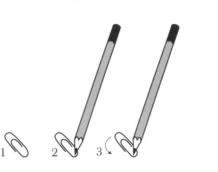

Predict: If you spin the paper clip 10 times, how many times do you think it will point at you when it stops?

Experiment: Spin the paper clip 10 times. Record your results.

Predict: What do you think will happen if you do it again 10 times? Try it.

Using this assessment task: Although the task may be done in a large group, more detailed assessment can be gathered in small groups. The teacher can more closely observe students conducting the experiment and probe into the reasoning behind their predictions.

Students should work on a smooth, flat surface. Each student will need a large (preferably plastic coated) paper clip, a pencil, and a sheet of paper to record results. Prior to beginning the task, demonstrate the spin. This demonstration works well shown on an overhead projector.

The experiment requires some manual dexterity to perform. To encourage students to hold the pencil steady while spinning the paper clip, the teacher could suggest that they draw a dot on their page and hold the point of the pencil on the dot while they spin the paper clip. A spinner could be used for this task; however, the less-structured paper-clip spin allows the teacher to observe how students determine whether the paper clip points at them and whether they attempt to skew the results subjectively in their favor by moving their bodies or the paper clip in some way.

In addition to performing the physical aspect of the experiment, students will need to devise a means to record their results. That is, they need to keep track of ten spins and keep track of how many of those ten spins pointed at themselves. Allow students to determine for themselves how they will keep track of the spins. Some students may neglect the recordkeeping portion of the task unless they are reminded or unless they are given some suggestions for how to make records. If prompting is required, some suggestions might be (a) to use counters that the student could place in a yes or no pile; (b) to list the numbers from 1 to 10 on a page and write "yes" or "no" or place a checkmark beside those spins that point to the student; or (c) to create a chart with two columns labeled "toward me" and "away from me" and make tally marks under the columns until they reach a total of ten tallies.

The prediction of how many times the paper clip will point toward the student indicates the student's understanding of chance. Although little emphasis is placed on assessing the first prediction, students with strong understanding will realize that it will likely point to them fewer than half the time (i.e., fewer than five times). The prediction at the end of the task—"What do you think will happen if you do it again?"—indicates whether the student is able to use the information from the experiment to make a better prediction. Once a student has made a prediction, the teacher can glean worthwhile information by asking, "Why did you choose that number?" Stronger students will base their choice on the results of the first experiment. Less-experienced students tend to pick their favorite numbers.

Solution: During the experiment the student makes the determination of whether the paper clip points toward herself or himself. Students should use consistent rules to make that decision. Many young learners are tempted to alter the rules so that the results match their prediction more accurately.

Keeping track of the results can be done in a number of ways. The main components include keeping track of the total number of spins to ten and the number of spins that point toward the player. Below are some possible methods:

Example 1

First prediction: 5

1. ✓   2. ✗   3. ✗   4. ✓   5. ✓   6. ✗   7. ✗   8. ✗   9. ✓   10. ✗

Result: 4 toward me.
Second prediction: 4, because that's what I got last time and because it's more likely that it will point away from me because there is more space away from me.

Example 2

First prediction: 8 to me.

| Toward me | ||| | 3 |
| Not toward me | |||||||| | 7 |

Second prediction: 4, because I guessed way too high the first time. It doesn't point to me very often.

Continuum of Understanding

	Initial Understanding	Developing Understanding	Strong Understanding
Experiment	Does not use consistent rules to determine whether the paper clip points toward himself or herself; adjusts body, manipulates results, or adjusts rules to try to match the prediction	Generally uses consistent rules to determine whether the paper clip is pointed toward himself or herself	Develops clear rules and uses them consistently throughout the ten trials
Data-collection strategies	Does not develop an effective means to keep track of trials or results, for example, may spin the paper clip many times until it points to himself or herself ten times but does not know the total number of spins	Chooses an appropriate strategy with some prompting to keep track of trials and results; may make some errors (e.g., may do slightly more or fewer than ten trials)	Chooses appropriate and efficient means to keep track of the number of trials to ten, and accurately records the number of times the paper clip pointed toward himself or herself
Predictions	Makes initial prediction that may be high, but does not use the results of the experiment to adjust his or her prediction the second time	Makes initial prediction that may be high; may then adjust the second prediction but be unable to articulate why the adjustment was made or why it was fewer than he or she initially thought	Makes initial prediction of five or fewer, then bases the second prediction on the results of the first experiment and justifies the prediction using the language of uncertainty (e.g., "it will be about four because my body takes up less space")

Looking for Evidence of Understanding

The skills involved in this task are related, but as Balo's and Jenn's work shows, students may demonstrate strong data-collection strategies but still be developing their understanding of chance.

Jasmyn

Experiment, Data Collection, and Predictions: Initial Understanding

Jasmyn did not keep track of the total number of spins. Instead, she printed the numeral for each time the paper clip pointed at her and continued spinning until she reached 10. She said, "Those numbers make it point at me." The teacher demonstrated the experiment after noticing her misunderstanding, but Jasmyn repeated the same procedure the second time. Because Jasmyn did not understand the experiment, her predictions were both "10." She viewed 10 as the target rather than as the number of trials.

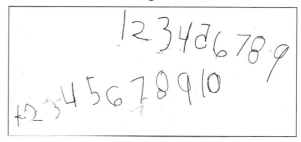

Balo

Experiment and Predictions: Initial Understanding

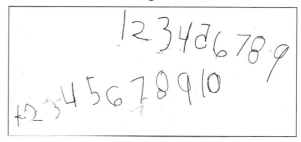

Balo wanted the paper clip to point at her and was sad when it did not do so. She commented, "It doesn't like me." After a few trials, she started to manipulate the results by not counting some trials that pointed away from her, adjusting her body so that the paper clip counted as pointing toward her, and moving the paper clip when she thought no one was looking. Her first prediction was 8. Disappointed that she didn't meet that goal, she recorded her second prediction as 1, but changed it to 100 after she had recorded two trials that pointed toward her early on. She tried the experiment a third time and wrote "102" as her prediction. When the teacher asked if that outcome was really possible, she changed it to "8," showing that she did not use the information gathered from the previous two experiments.

Data Collection Strategies: Strong Understanding

Balo created a two-column chart and marked down her result after each trial. Periodically she counted how many happy faces she had recorded and determined how many more were needed.

Jenn

Experiment and Data Collection: Strong Understanding

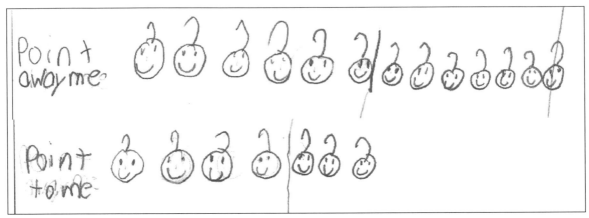

Jenn used the sides of her body as indicators of the range in which the paper clip had to land. At the bottom of the page (not shown), Jenn wrote the numbers from 1 to 10. After each trial she added a face to her picture graph and erased the next number in the sequence until she had erased all ten numbers.

Predictions: Developing Understanding

Jenn's prediction for the first experiment was high (8). Although she adjusted her prediction for the second trial to 3, she said it was because she "only got four last time" but could not articulate further why her prediction should be lower.

Variations for the Range of Learners

Working in pairs may be useful for less-experienced students. That arrangement allows one person to do the spinning and the other person to record the results. Having two students work together typically leads to more formal negotiations of the rules of the experiment and fewer occurrences of "cheating." The teacher may want to structure the data collection more directly by providing ten counters and a master chart showing two circles labeled "toward me" and "away from me." After each trial, the student places a counter or chip in one of the two circles. This approach ensures that ten trials are completed and reminds students of the two possible outcomes. To make the task more challenging, pairs of students could conduct the experiment with three outcomes, that is, "toward Justin," "toward Daniel," and "toward no one."

Blackline Masters

Number Cards: Sheet 1

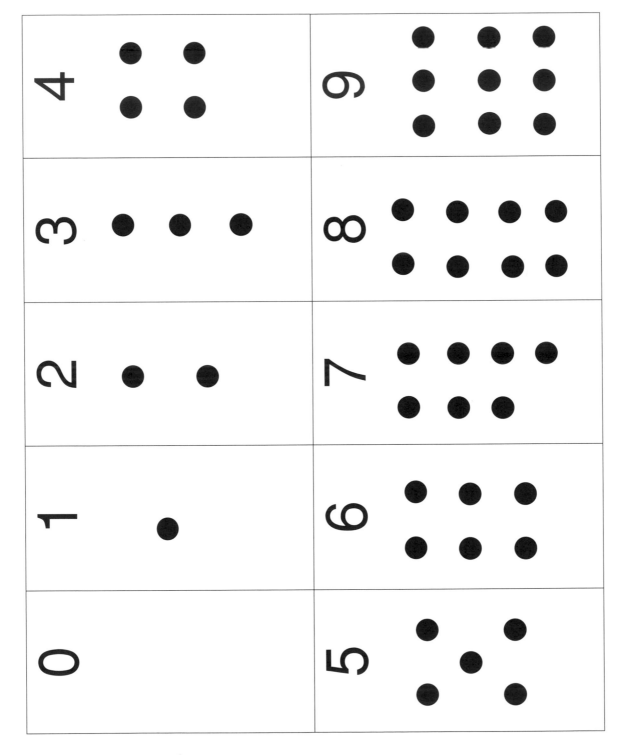

Number Cards: Sheet 2

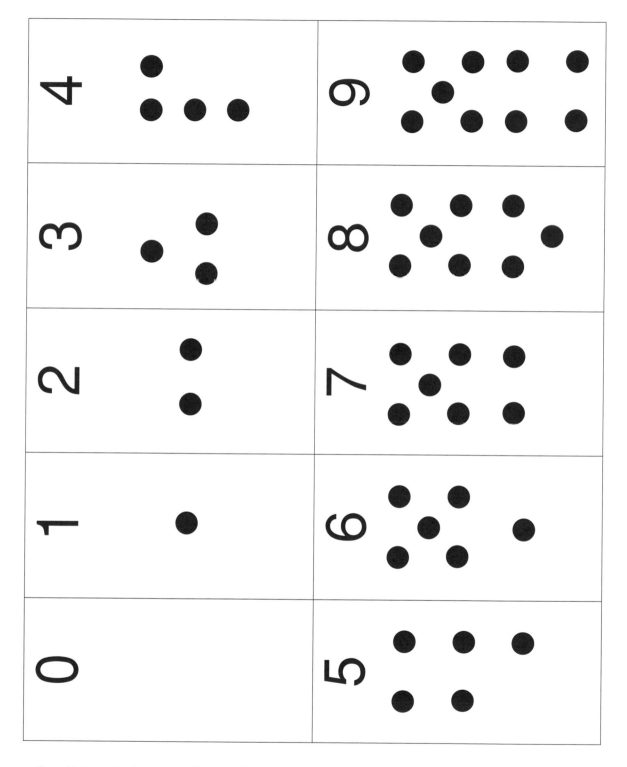

What Comes Next? Observation Form

Student name _____   Date _____

	Yes	No	Comments
Adds next piece in pattern			
Is able to continue the pattern with additional pieces			
Demonstrates an understanding of how the pattern works			
Articulates why specified pieces were added to the pattern			
Describes the repeating core of the pattern			

Student name _____   Date _____

	Yes	No	Comments
Adds next piece in pattern			
Is able to continue the pattern with additional pieces			
Demonstrates an understanding of how the pattern works			
Articulates why specified pieces were added to the pattern			
Describes the repeating core of the pattern			

Making Patterns: Observation Form

Student	Two patterns that student generates	No. of times core repeats	Is pattern predictable?	What is the same?	What is different?

From *Mathematics Assessment Sampler, Prekindergarten–Grade 2*, edited by DeAnn Huinker and Anne M. Collins. Copyright © 2006 The National Council of Teachers of Mathematics, Inc., www.nctm.org. All rights reserved. May be photocopied for personal or classroom distribution only. For permission to copy or distribute this material for all other purposes, please contact Copyright Clearance Center, www.copyright.com.

Algebra
Fixing Patterns

Name _____   Date _____

I made a pattern by snapping together 12 connecting cubes. Then it fell apart.
All I have left of my pattern are 3 of the cubes I snapped together. They look
like this.

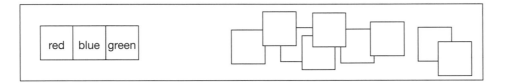

Draw a picture of what my pattern might have looked like.

Might it have looked any other way? Describe your thinking, and show another
possibility if one exists.

Algebra
Growing Creature

Name _____   Date _____

1. On day 1, 5 squares are needed to build the creature. It grows the same amount each day. What will it look like on day 2 and on day 3?

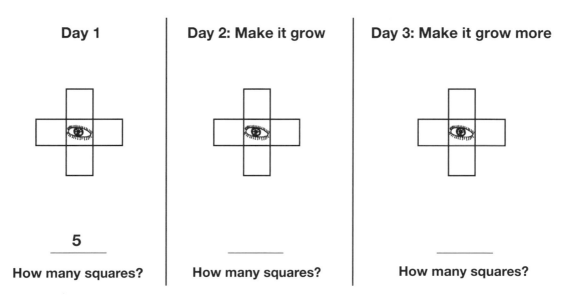

Day 1	**Day 2: Make it grow**	**Day 3: Make it grow more**
5	_____	_____
How many squares?	**How many squares?**	**How many squares?**

2. How many squares will the creature have on day 4? _____

3. Look at the creature you made. Use words, numbers, or diagrams, or a combination of those ways, to describe how you made your creature grow. Tell about the patterns you see in the shapes and numbers.

Algebra
How Much Is It Worth?

Name _____   Date _____

Use triangles and hexagons from a set of pattern blocks to solve this problem. Use pictures, numbers, or words, or a combination of those ways, to explain your thinking.

1. If 1 triangle is worth 2¢, how much is 1 hexagon worth?

2. What happens if 1 triangle is worth 5¢? How much is 1 hexagon worth?

3. How much are 2 hexagons worth?

Algebra
What Goes in the ☐?

Name _____   Date _____

What number would you put in the ☐ to make this a true number sentence?

$$8 + 4 = \boxed{} + 5$$

How did you figure out your answer?

Algebra
True and False Number Sentences

Name _____   Date _____

For each number sentence, tell whether it is true or false. How do you know?

a. $5 + 4 = 9$ True   False

b. $9 = 5 + 4$ True   False

c. $9 = 9$ True   False

Algebra
True and False Number Sentences—Continued

d.   5 + 4 = 4 + 5   True   False

e.   5 + 4 = 5 + 4   True   False

f.   5 + 4 = 6 + 3   True   False

g.   5 + 5 = 5 + 6   True   False

Geometry
Quick Images

Name _____   Date _____

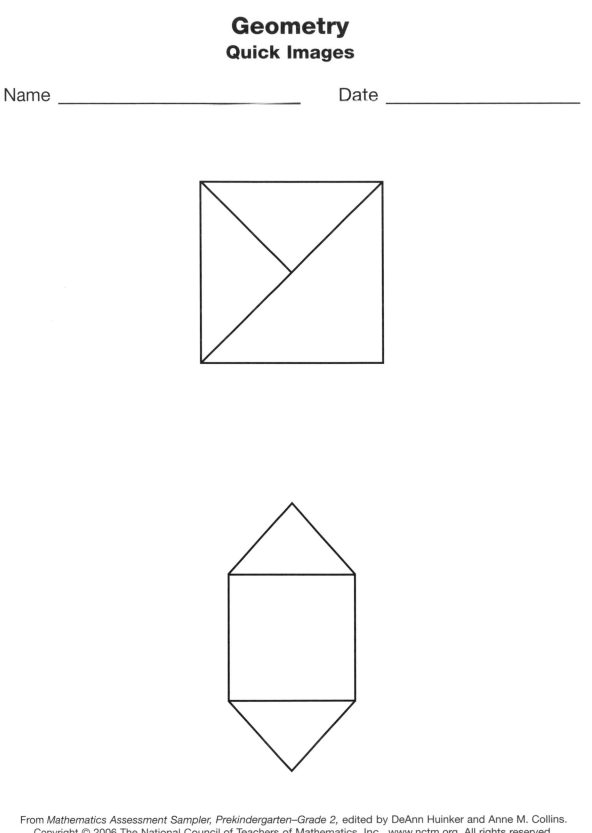

Geometry
All about Triangles

Name _____   Date _____

Mark all the triangles on the page. Tell how you know that they are triangles?

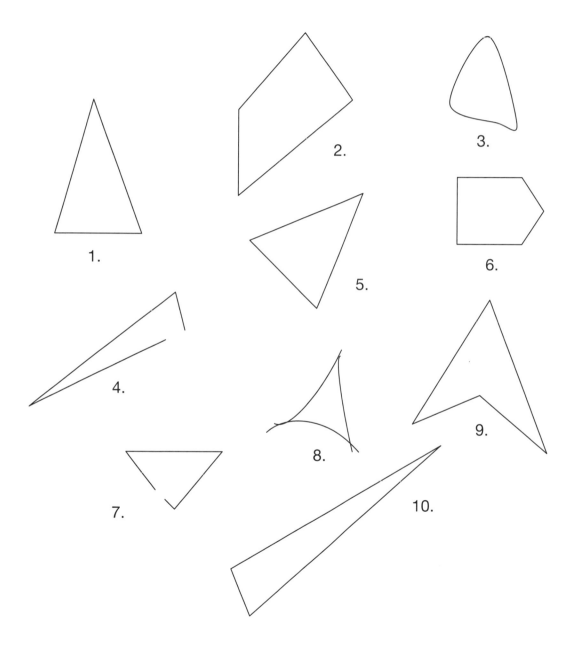

Geometry
Comparing Shapes

Name _____   Date _____

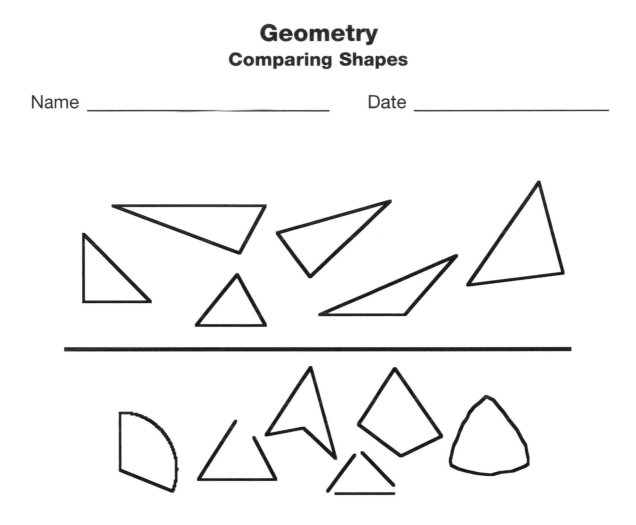

The shapes above the line are all alike. How are they different from the ones below the line?

Geometry
Squareville

Name _____   Date _____

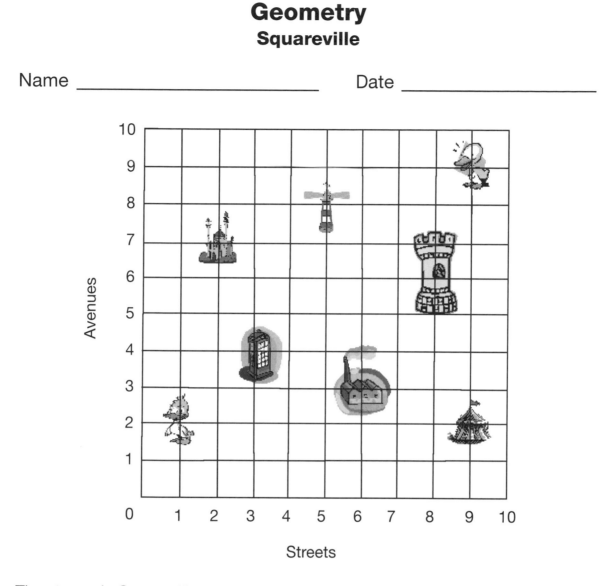

The streets in Squareville are numbered 0 to 10 and run left to right. The avenues are also numbered 0 to 10 and run from bottom to top.

1. Give Mr. Duck directions that he can follow to get to Mr. Quack. Mr. Duck is at location (1, 2) and Mr. Quack is at location (9, 9).

2. Describe another way to get Mr. Duck to Mr. Quack.

Geometry
Aunt Sally's Cookies

Name _____   Date _____

Aunt Sally likes to make interesting shaped cookies for her nephews Billy and Bob. To get a cookie, they have to tell her how to make one cut in the cookie so that they each get a fair share. Show Aunt Sally how to cut each cookie into two pieces that are the exact same size and shape. Billy will receive one piece and Bob will receive one piece.

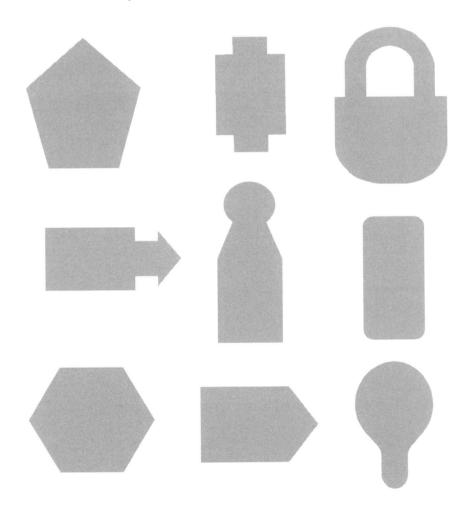

Could Aunt Sally cut any of the cookies in more than one way? If so, explain how.

Geometry
Shapes in Motion

Name _____ Date _____

Color in and then cut out these shapes.

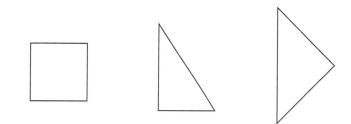

The shape on the "start" side was moved so that it ended up in the "finish" position. Use the shapes you cut out to show how the shape moved. Then describe how the shape moved to get from the start to the finish.

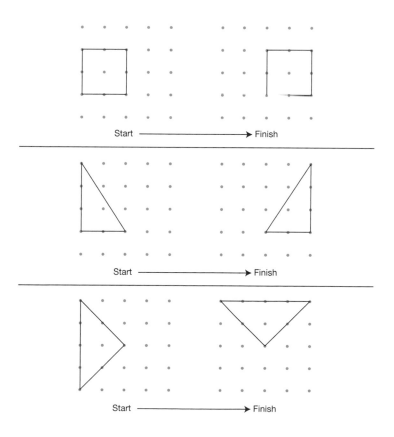

Measurement
Before and After

Name _____ Date _____

Tell me what might happen before you leave school. How did you decide?

Tell me what might happen after you leave school. How did you decide?

Before   After

Measurement
Before and After

Name _____   Date _____

Tell me what might happen before lunch. How did you decide?

Tell me what might happen after lunch. How did you decide?

Before   After

Measurement
Before and After

Name _____   Date _____

Tell me what might happen before recess? How did you decide?

Tell me what might happen after recess? How did you decide?

Before   After

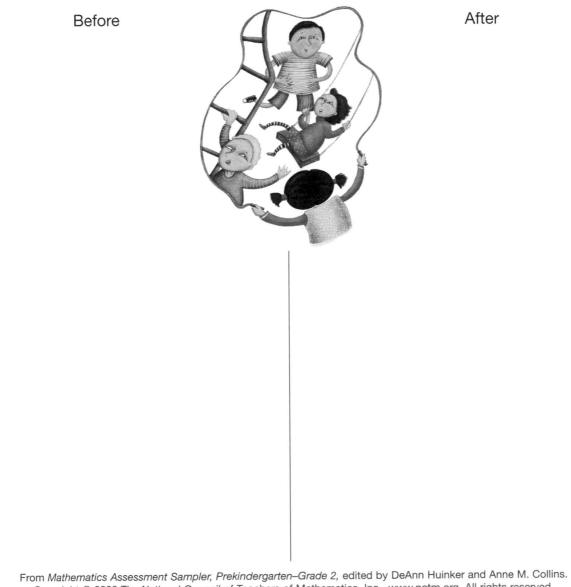

Measurement
Before and After: Observation Form

Name _____   Date _____

Prompt	Before		After	
	Event	Explanation	Event	Explanation
A				
B				
C				

Name _____   Date _____

Prompt	Before		After	
	Event	Explanation	Event	Explanation
A				
B				
C				

Measurement
Is This Possible?

Name _____ Date _____

Look at picture 1. Is this situation possible or impossible? Tell me why you think it is possible or not possible.

Picture 1

Look at picture 2. Is this situation possible? Tell me why you think it is possible or not possible.

Picture 2

Measurement
Six Straws: Checklist

Name _____ Date _____

First Unit Criteria	Y–Yes; S–Somewhat; N–No
Makes a reasonable estimate for the first unit	
Communicates a useful estimation method	
Applies appropriate measuring technique by lining up units without gaps or overlaps	
Is able to determine whether estimation is too long or too short in the process of measuring	

Second Unit Criteria	Y–Yes; S–Somewhat; N–No
Makes a reasonable estimate for the second unit by using the information gained from the first measuring task.	
Communicates that the distance is longer/shorter because the units are longer/shorter	
Applies appropriate measuring technique	
Is able to determine whether the estimate is too long or too short in the process of measuring	

Anecdotal Comments:

Measurement
More Time—Less Time

Name _____   Date _____

Measurement
More Time—Less Time:
Observation Form

Name _____   Date _____

Understands Problem	Level of Understanding	Explanations	Anecdotal Comments
Complete understanding			
Partial understanding			
Misunderstanding			
Solves Problem			
Orders all destinations correctly			
Orders some of the destinations correctly			
Is unsuccessful at ordering the destinations			
Communicates Reasoning			
Gives clear, concise, and correct explanation			
Gives good but not completely clear explanation			
Gives insufficient explanation			

Alphabet Letters Sort

A	B	C	D
E	F	G	H
I	J	K	L
M	N	O	P
Q	R	S	T
U	V	W	X
Y	Z		

Is It Likely? Category Cards

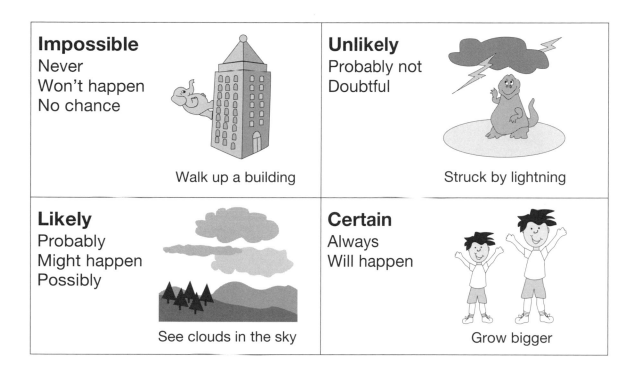

Impossible
Never
Won't happen
No chance

Walk up a building

Unlikely
Probably not
Doubtful

Struck by lightning

Likely
Probably
Might happen
Possibly

See clouds in the sky

Certain
Always
Will happen

Grow bigger

Is It Likely? Event Cards

Name _____   Date _____

It will snow tomorrow.	You will have 2 birthdays this year.
A rock will sink when it is dropped into a glass of water.	The sky will be green tomorrow.
Everyone will be in class tomorrow.	You will have spaghetti for supper.
Touching fire will burn you.	You will read a book tonight.

Is It Likely? Event Cards—*Continued*

Name _____   Date _____

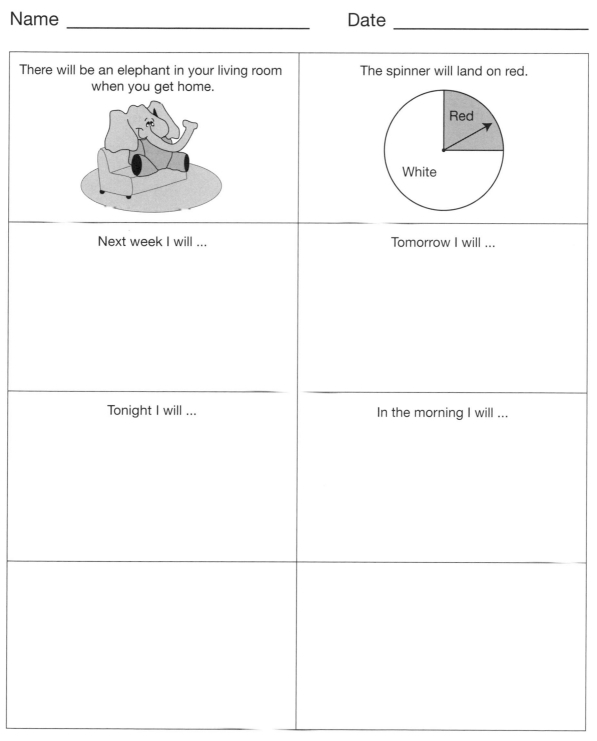

There will be an elephant in your living room when you get home.	The spinner will land on red.
Next week I will ...	Tomorrow I will ...
Tonight I will ...	In the morning I will ...

Data Analysis and Probability
Picking Possibilities

Name _____   Date _____

1. **Understand:** Combinations	2. **Experiment:** Pick two sticks			
	1		6	
	2		7	
	3		8	
	4		9	
	5		10	

3. Organize Results

4. Interpret: Which color pairs are most likely? Least likely? Why do you think so?

_____

_____

_____

_____

_____

Data Analysis and Probability
Do You Have All the Information You Need?

Name _____   Date _____

A group of second graders made this graph. It tells you something about their class.

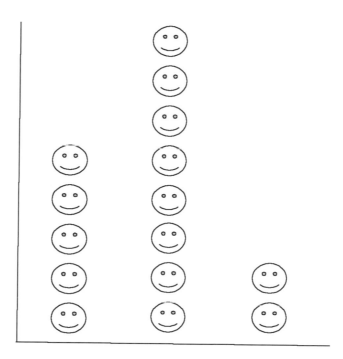

What might the graph tell you about this class?

What information is missing that would help you find out about the class?

Appendix:
Items Matrices

Number and Operations Items Matrix, Chapter 1

Assessment Item Number	1	2	3	4	5	6	7	8	9	10	11	12
Content Standards and Expectations: Number and Operations												
Understand numbers, ways of representing numbers, relationships among numbers, and number systems												
Count with understanding and recognize "how many" in sets of objects	X	X	X									
Use multiple models to develop initial understandings of place value and the base-ten number system							X					
Develop understanding of the relative position and magnitude of whole numbers and of ordinal and cardinal numbers and their connections	X	X	X									
Develop a sense of whole numbers and represent and use them in flexible ways, including relating, composing, and decomposing numbers					X				X			
Connect number words and numerals to the quantities they represent, using various physical models and representations	X	X	X									
Understand and represent commonly used fractions, such as 1/4, 1/3, and 1/2										X		
Understand meanings of operations and how they relate to one another												
Understand various meanings of addition and subtraction of whole numbers and the relationship between the two operations				X		X	X	X	X	X	X	X
Understand the effects of adding and subtracting whole numbers					X			X	X			
Understand situations that entail multiplication and division, such as equal groupings of objects and sharing equally										X	X	X
Compute fluently and make reasonable estimates												
Develop and use strategies for whole-number computations, with a focus on addition and subtraction				X	X	X	X					
Develop fluency with basic number combinations for addition and subtraction												
Use a variety of methods and tools to compute, including objects, mental computation, estimation, paper and pencil, and calculators				X		X	X	X		X	X	
Process Standards												
Problem Solving	X			X	X	X	X	X	X	X	X	X
Communication		X	X	X	X	X	X	X	X	X	X	X
Reasoning and Proof		X	X	X	X	X	X	X	X	X	X	X
Connections	X			X		X	X	X	X	X	X	X
Representation				X	X	X	X	X	X	X	X	X
Grade Range	Pre-K–1	Pre-K–1	Pre-K–1	K–2	K–2	K–2	1–2	1–2	1–2	1–2	1–2	1–2

Algebra Items Matrix, Chapter 2

Assessment Item Number	1	2	3	4	5	6	7
Content Standards and Expectations: Algebra							
Understand patterns, relations, and functions							
Sort, classify, and order objects by size, number, and other properties	X						
Recognize, describe, and extend patterns such as sequences of sounds and shapes or simple numeric patterns and translate from one representation to another		X					
Analyze how both repeating and growing patterns are generated			X	X			
Represent and analyze mathematical situations and structures using algebraic symbols							
Illustrate general principles and properties of operations, such as commutativity, using specific numbers							X
Use concrete, pictorial, and verbal representations to develop an understanding of invented and conventional symbolic notations						X	X
Use mathematical models to represent and understand quantitative relationships							
Model situations that involve the addition and subtraction of whole numbers, using objects, pictures, and symbols							
Analyze change in various contexts							
Describe qualitative change, such as a student's growing taller							
Describe quantitative change, such as a student's growing two inches in one year					X		
Process Standards							
Problem Solving	X	X	X	X	X		
Communication	X	X	X	X	X	X	X
Reasoning and Proof	X	X	X	X	X	X	X
Connections		X					
Representation			X	X			
Grade Range	Pre-K–K	K–2	K–2	K–2	1–2	1–2	1–2

Geometry Items Matrix, Chapter 3

Assessment Item Number	1	2	3	4	5	6	7	8
Content Standards and Expectations: Geometry								
Analyze characteristics and properties of two- and three-dimensional geometric shapes and develop mathematical arguments about geometric relationships								
Recognize, name, build, draw, compare, and sort two- and three-dimensional shapes			X	X	X			
Describe attributes and parts of two- and three-dimensional shapes				X	X			
Investigate and predict the results of putting together and taking apart two- and three-dimensional shapes								
Specify locations and describe spatial relationships using coordinate geometry and other representational systems								
Describe, name, and interpret relative positions in space and apply ideas about relative position	X					X		
Describe, name, and interpret direction and distance in navigating space and apply ideas about direction and distance								
Find and name locations with simple relationships such as "near to" and in coordinate systems such as maps						X		
Apply transformations and use symmetry to analyze mathematical situations								
Recognize and apply slides, flips, and turns							X	X
Recognize and create shapes that have symmetry								
Use visualization, spatial reasoning, and geometric modeling to solve problems								
Create mental images of geometric shapes using spatial memory and spatial visualization		X						
Recognize and represent shapes from different perspectives								
Relate ideas in geometry to ideas in number and measurement								
Recognize geometric shapes and structures in the environment and specify their location								
Process Standards								
Problem Solving								
Communication	X	X	X	X	X	X		X
Reasoning and Proof	X	X	X	X	X	X	X	X
Connections						X	X	
Representation		X					X	
Grade Range	Pre-K–K	Pre-K–2	Pre-K–2	K–2	1–2	1–2	1–2	1–2

Measurement Items Matrix, Chapter 4

Assessment Item Number	1	2	3	4	5	6	7	8	9
Content Standards and Expectations: Measurement									
Understand measurable attributes of objects and the units, systems, and processes of measurement									
Recognize the attributes of length, volume, weight, area, and time	X	X	X	X	X	X	X	X	
Compare and order objects according to these attributes		X	X	X	X		X		
Understand how to measure using nonstandard and standard units	X					X	X		
Select an appropriate unit and tool for the attribute being measured									
Apply appropriate techniques, tools, and formulas to determine measurements									
Measure with multiple copies of units of the same size, such as paper clips laid end to end						X			
Use repetition of a single unit to measure something larger than the unit, for instance, measuring the length of a room with a single meterstick									X
Use tools to measure									X
Develop common referents for measures to make comparisons and estimates			X						
Process Standards									
Problem Solving									
Communication	X	X	X	X	X	X	X	X	X
Reasoning and Proof	X	X	X	X	X	X	X		
Connections								X	
Representation									
Grade Range	Pre-K–1	Pre-K–1	Pre-K–1	Pre-K–1	Pre-K–1	Pre-K–2	Pre-K–2	K–1	K–2

Data Analysis and Probability Items Matrix, Chapter 5

Assessment Item Number	1	2	3	4	5	6	7	8	9
Content Standards and Expectations: Data Analysis and Probability									
Formulate questions that can be addressed with data and collect, organize, and display relevant data to answer them									
Pose questions and gather data about themselves and their surroundings				X	X				X
Sort and classify objects according to their attributes and organize data about the objects	X						X		
Represent data using concrete objects, pictures, and graphs	X				X		X		
Select and use appropriate statistical methods to analyze data									
Describe parts of the data and the set of data as a whole to determine what the data show	X				X		X	X	
Develop and evaluate inferences and predictions that are based on data									
Discuss events related to students' experiences as likely or unlikely		X	X			X	X		X
Understand and apply basic concepts of probability									
Process Standards									
Problem Solving									
Communication	X	X	X	X	X	X	X	X	X
Reasoning and Proof	X	X	X			X	X		X
Connections		X			X				
Representation	X		X	X	X		X		X
Grade Range	Pre-K–2	Pre-K–2	Pre-K–2	K–2	K–2	K–2	K–2	1–2	1–2

Bibliography

Carpenter, Thomas P., Megan L. Franke, and Linda Levi. *Thinking Mathematically: Integrating Arithmetic and Algebra in Elementary School.* Portsmouth, N.H.: Heinemann, 2003.

Crowley, Mary L. "The van Hiele Model of the Development of Geometric Thought." In *Learning and Teaching Geometry, K–12: 1987 Yearbook,* edited by Mary Montgomery Lindquist, pp. 1–16. Reston, Va.: National Council of Teachers of Mathematics, 1987.

Dacey, Linda, Mary Cavanagh, Carol R. Findell, Carole E. Greenes, Linda Jensen Sheffield, and Marian Small. *Navigating through Measurement in Prekindergarten–Grade 2. Principles and Standards for School Mathematics* Navigations Series. Reston, Va.: National Council of Teachers of Mathematics, 2003.

Department of Education, Employment, and Training. *Early Numeracy Interview Booklet.* Melbourne, Victoria, Australia: State Government Victoria, 2001.

Economopoulos, Karen, Jan Mokros, and Susan Jo Russell. *From Paces to Feet: Measuring and Data.* Palo Alto, Calif.: Dale Seymour Publications, 1999.

Findell, Carol R., Marian Small, Mary Cavanagh, Linda Dacey, Carole E. Greenes, and Linda Jensen Sheffield. *Navigating through Geometry in Prekindergarten–Grade 2. Principles and Standards for School Mathematics* Navigations Series. Reston, Va.: National Council of Teachers of Mathematics, 2001.

Glanfield, Florence, William S. Bush, and Jean Kerr Stenmark, eds. *Mathematics Assessment: A Practical Handbook for Grades K–2.* Reston, Va.: National Council of Teachers of Mathematics, 2003.

Greenes, Carole E., Mary Cavanagh, Linda Dacey, Carol R. Findell, and Marian Small. *Navigating through Algebra in Prekindergarten–Grade 2. Principles and Standards for School Mathematics* Navigations Series. Reston, Va.: National Council of Teachers of Mathematics, 2001.

National Council of Teachers of Mathematics (NCTM). *Curriculum and Evaluation Standards for School Mathematics.* Reston, Va.: NCTM, 1989.

———. *Assessment Standards for School Mathematics.* Reston, Va.: NCTM, 1995.

———. *Principles and Standards for School Mathematics.* Reston, Va.: NCTM, 2000.

Sources for Assessment Items

Ann Arbor Public Schools. *Alternative Assessment: Evaluating Student Performance in Elementary Mathematics.* Palo Alto, Calif.: Dale Seymour Publications, 1993.

Braddon, Kathryn L., Nancy J. Hall, and Dale B. Taylor. *Math through Children's Literature: Making the NCTM Standards Come Alive.* Portsmouth, N.H.: Teacher Ideas Press, 1993.

Bryant, Deborah, and Mark Driscoll. *Exploring Classroom Assessment in Mathematics: A Guide for Professional Development.* Reston, Va.: National Council of Teachers of Mathematics, 1998.

Bush, William S., ed. *Mathematics Assessment: Cases and Discussion Questions for Grades K–5.* Reston, Va.: National Council of Teachers of Mathematics, 2001.

Carpenter, Thomas P., Megan L. Franke, and Linda Levi. *Thinking Mathematically: Integrating Arithmetic and Algebra in Elementary School.* Portsmouth, N.H.: Heinemann, 2003.

Cavanagh, Mary, Linda Dacey, Carol R. Findell, Carole E. Greenes, Linda Jensen Sheffield, and Marian Small. *Navigating through Number and Operations in Prekindergarten–Grade 2. Principles and Standards for School Mathematics* Navigations Series. Reston, Va.: National Council of Teachers of Mathematics, 2004.

Center for Performance Assessment. *Classroom Tips and Tools for Busy Teachers (Elementary Edition).* Performance Assessment Series. Denver: Advance Learning Press, 2001.

Clements, Douglas H. "Subitizing: What Is It? Why Teach It?" *Teaching Children Mathematics* 5 (March 1999): 400–405.

Clements, Douglas, and Julie Sarama. "The Earliest Geometry." *Teaching Children Mathematics* 7 (October 2000): 82–86.

Clements, Douglas, Julie Sarama, and Ann-Marie DiBiase. "Preschool and Kindergarten Mathematics: A National Conference." *Teaching Children Mathematics* 8 (May 2002): 510–14.

———, eds. *Engaging Young Children in Mathematics: Standards for Early Childhood Mathematics Education.* Mahwah, N.J.: Lawrence Erlbaum Associates, 2004.

Copley, Juanita V. *The Young Child and Mathematics*. Reston, Va.: National Council of Teachers of Mathematics, and Washington, D.C.: National Association for the Education of Young Children, 2000.

———, ed. *Showcasing Mathematics for the Young Child: Activities for Three-, Four-, and Five-Year-Olds*. Reston, Va.: National Council of Teachers of Mathematics, and Washington, D.C.: National Association for the Education of Young Children, 2004.

Copley, Juanita V., Kristin Glass, Linda Nix, Alison Faseler, Maria De Jesus, and Sheila Tanksley. "Measuring Experiences for Young Children." *Teaching Children Mathematics* 10 (February 2004): 314–19.

Crowley, Mary L. "The van Hiele Model of the Development of Geometric Thought." In *Learning and Teaching Geometry, K–12: 1987 Yearbook*, edited by Mary Montgomery Lindquist, pp. 1–16. Reston, Va.: National Council of Teachers of Mathematics, 1987.

Department of Education, Employment, and Training. *Early Numeracy Interview Booklet*. Melbourne, Victoria, Australia: State Government Victoria, 2001.

Evans, Caroline W., Anne J. Leija, and Trina R. Falkner. *Math Links: Teaching the NCTM 2000 Standards through Children's Literature*. Portsmouth, N.H.: Teacher Ideas Press, 2001.

Falkner, Karen P., Linda Levi, and Thomas P. Carpenter. "Children's Understanding of Equality: A Foundation for Algebra." *Teaching Children Mathematics* 6 (December 1999): 232–36.

Findell, Carol R., Marian Small, Mary Cavanagh, Linda Dacey, Carole E. Greenes, and Linda Jensen Sheffield. *Navigating through Geometry in Prekindergarten–Grade 2. Principles and Standards for School Mathematics* Navigations Series. Reston, Va.: National Council of Teachers of Mathematics, 2001.

Fosnot, Catherine T., and Maarten Dolk. *Young Mathematicians at Work: Constructing Number Sense, Addition, and Subtraction*. Portsmouth, N.H.: Heinemann, 2001.

Fuson, Karen C., Laura Grandau, and Patricia A. Sugiyama. "Achievable Numerical Understandings for All Young Children." *Teaching Children Mathematics* 7 (May 2001): 522–26.

Glanfield, Florence, William S. Bush, and Jean Kerr Stenmark, eds. *Mathematics Assessment: A Practical Handbook for Grades K–2*. Reston, Va.: National Council of Teachers of Mathematics, 2003.

Goodrow, Anne, Douglas H. Clements, Michael T. Battista, Julie Sarama, and Joan Akers. *How Long? How Far?* White Plains, N.Y.: Dale Seymour Publications, 1998.

Greenes, Carole E., Mary Cavanagh, Linda Dacey, Carol R. Findell, and Marian Small. *Navigating through Algebra in Prekindergarten–Grade 2. Principles and Standards for School Mathematics* Navigations Series. Reston, Va.: National Council of Teachers of Mathematics, 2001.

Griffin, Sharon. "Laying the Foundation for Computational Fluency in Early Childhood." *Teaching Children Mathematics* 9 (February 2003): 306–9.

Hannibal, Mary Anne. "Young Children's Developing Understanding of Geometric Shapes." *Teaching Children Mathematics* 5 (February 1999): 353–57.

Myren, Christina. *Posing Open-Ended Questions in the Primary Classroom.* San Diego, Calif.: Teaching Resource Center, 1995.

National Council of Teachers of Mathematics (NCTM). *Assessment Standards for School Mathematics.* Reston, Va.: NCTM, 1995.

———. *Principles and Standards for School Mathematics.* Reston, Va.: NCTM, 2000.

———. "Early Childhood Mathematics: Promoting Good Beginnings." NCTM Position Statement. *Teaching Children Mathematics* 9 (September 2002): 24.

Pandey, Tej. *A Sampler of Mathematics Assessment.* Sacramento, Calif.: California Department of Education, 1991.

Sanford, Susan. "Assessing Measurement in the Primary Classroom." In *Assessment in the Mathematics Classroom: 1993 Yearbook,* edited by Norman L. Webb, pp. 74–79. Reston, Va.: National Council of Teachers of Mathematics, 1993.

Sheffield, Linda Jensen, Mary Cavanagh, Linda Dacey, Carol R. Findell, Carole E. Greenes, and Marian Small. *Navigating through Data Analysis and Probability in Prekindergarten–Grade 2. Principles and Standards for School Mathematics* Navigations Series. Reston, Va.: National Council of Teachers of Mathematics, 2002.

St. Clair, James. "Assessing Mathematical Understanding in a Bilingual Kindergarten." In *Assessment in the Mathematics Classroom: 1993 Yearbook,* edited by Norman L. Webb, pp. 65–73. Reston, Va.: National Council of Teachers of Mathematics, 1993.

Stenmark, Jean Kerr, ed. *Mathematics Assessment: Myths, Models, Good Questions, and Practical Suggestions.* Reston, Va.: National Council of Teachers of Mathematics, 1991.

Sullivan, Peter, and Pat Lilburn. *Good Questions for Math Teaching: Why Ask Them and What to Ask, K–6.* Sausalito, Calif.: Math Solutions Publications, 2002.

Tierney, Cornelia, and Susan Jo Russell. *Ten-Minute Math.* Parsippany, N.J.: Dale Seymour Publications, 2001.

Victoria Department of Education, Employment and Training. *Early Numeracy Interview Booklet*. Melbourne, Victoria, Australia: State of Victoria, 2001.

Woleck, Kristine Reed. "Tricky Triangles: A Tale of One, Two, Three Researchers." *Teaching Children Mathematics* 10 (September 2003): 40–44.

Wright, Tracey, Jan Mokros, and Susan Jo Russell. *Bigger, Taller, Heavier, Smaller*. White Plains, N.Y.: Dale Seymour Publications, 1998.

Three additional titles appear in the Mathematics Assessment Samplers series

(Anne M. Collins, series editor)

✪ *Mathematics Assessment Sampler, Grades 3–5, Items Aligned with NCTM's* Principles and Standards for School Mathematics,
edited by Jane D. Gawronski

✪ *Mathematics Assessment Sampler, Grades 6–8, Items Aligned with NCTM's* Principles and Standards for School Mathematics,
edited by John Burrill

✪ *Mathematics Assessment Sampler, Grades 9–12, Items Aligned with NCTM's* Principles and Standards for School Mathematics,
edited by Betty Travis

Please consult www.nctm.org/catalog for the availability of these titles, as well as for a plethora of resources for teachers of mathematics at all grade levels.

✪

For the most up-to-date listing of NCTM resources on topics of interest to mathematics educators, as well as information on membership benefits, conferences, and workshops, visit the NCTM Web site at www.nctm.org.